Dicks are Dumb

A Woman's Guide to Choosing the Right Man

MARY HONEYB MORRISON

Copyright © 2017 by Mary B. Morrison, Incorporated

All rights reserved. No part of this book may be reproduced in any form or by any means without the prior written consent of Mary B. Morrison, Incorporated, excepting brief quotes used in reviews or social media posts.

This title is available at special quantities discount for bulk purchased for sales promotion, premiums, fund-raising, educational or institutional use. Special book excerpts or customized printings can also be created to fit specific needs. For details, email or phone the office of Mary B. Morrison, Incorporated, Special Sales Department at TheRealMaryB@gmail.com or call 1-770-852-5069.

Library of Congress Card Catalogue Number: 1-5854370891

ISBN-13: 978-0-9674001-1-2
ISBN-10: 0-9674001-1-2
First Mary B. Morrison, Incorporated Trade Edition: November 2017

10 9 8 7 6 5 4 3 2 1

Printed in the United States of America

Cover Designed by: Richard C. Montgomery
Cover Photographer: AJ Alexander Parhm
Author Photo: AJ Alexander Parhm
Editors: Latoya C. Smith, Tanya Link, and Wendy Rogers-Curtis
Formatting by Elaine York, Allusion Graphics, LLC/Publishing and Book Formatting, www.allusiongraphics.com

Dicks are Dumb

Table of Contents

Introduction 1

I. WOMEN MUST THINK FOR THEMSELVES 13
    1 A Woman's Worth 15
    2 Value Your Vagina 27
    3 Baby Girls and Baby Dolls 41
    4 Interview with a Dick 50

II. THE THREE RINGS 63
    5 Relationship Ring 65
    6 Engagement Ring 71
    7 Wedding Ring 76

III. WHAT MEN WANT 83
    8 Why Men Cheat 85
    9 Sex Galore Doesn't Make Her a Whore 91
    10 Every Dick has a Dumb Moment 101

IV. WHOSE TEAM IS THIS DICK ON 109
    11 He's Bi-Sexual 111
    12 Sex Behind Bars 121
    13 He Doesn't Know 125
    14 Stop Dying for His Dick 127

V. THE DIVA AND THE DICK 133
    15 Good Dick is Mandatory 135
    16 The Mistress Gets Perks 146
    17 Divorcing the Dick 150

To every woman

Take charge of the love and happiness
you deserve in your relationships.

Acknowledgements

All praises to the divine power who loves us unconditionally, and gives us the power to choose whether we will love ourselves.

Also by Mary B. Morrison

The Crystal Series
Baby, You're The Best
Just Can't Let Go

If I Can't Have You Series
If I Can't Have You
I'd Rather Be With You
If You Don't Know Me

Soulmates Dissipate Series
Soulmates Dissipate
Never Again Once More
He's Just a Friend
Somebody's Gotta Be on Top
Nothing Has Ever Felt Like This
When Somebody Loves You Back
Darius Jones

The Honey Diaries
Sweeter Than Honey
Who's Loving You
Unconditionally Single
<u>*Darius Jones*</u>
She Ain't the One (coauthored with Carl Weber)
Maneater (anthology with Noire)
The Eternal Engagement
Justice Just Us Just Me
Who's Making Love

Mary B. Morrison, writing as HoneyB
Sexcapades
Single Husbands
Married on Mondays
The Rich Girls Club

Presented by Mary B. Morrison
Diverse Stories: From the Imaginations of Sixth Graders
(an anthology of fiction written by thirty-three 6th graders)

*A man with his hand out
needs to put his dick in it.*

Introduction

If a man's dick stops working, that bitch will lose his fucking mind.

Just when you think you've picked the right dick, he fucks up.

I'm a New York Times bestselling author, relationship sexpert, executive producer, speaker, instructor and creator of my *Vaginal Aerobics* and *Head Master* classes. I have twenty-three published fiction novels.

I've met a lot of dicks. When I converse with a man, I focus on understanding his relationship with his dick. The moment I tell a man that I write adult content—from the eight-five-year old white man at the golfing resort, to the ethnically diverse millennials—they immediately share the most intimate parts of their life. Proudly, I've answered numerous questions for men regarding health, sex, sexuality, and how to prevent erectile dysfunction.

If a man's woman/wife could hear his confessions to me, women would be shocked. A lot of men do not love or are not in-love with their main.

Based on what I've learned from men, I refuse to dumb down this book by censoring what needs to be said. If profanity offends you, I recommend you read my cleaner version of *Dicks Are Dumb: A Woman's Guide to Choosing the Right Man*, entitled, *Never Let a Man Come First*. Your mama probably never told you what your daddy has always known. Dicks respond to stimulation, not intellect.

A nice round ass, perky tits, thick lips, seductive moan, long or short hair, a whisper in his ear, or the scent of a woman walking by, will command his manhood's attention without a woman's knowledge or consent. Dicks do not have an IQ (Intelligence Quota). Dicks have a DIQ (Dumb Intelligence Quota) a subzero intellect. Now that you realize this, the only question is, "How dumb is his dick?"

Think about all the men you never thought would cheat on their beautiful, smart, and successful ladies, the mothers of their children, fiancées, or wives. One of those women might be you. Often, the woman a man cheats with is not more attractive than his woman/wife.

A man doesn't say, "Give me some of them good looks baby." His dick is on a mission ultimately to fuck. Men don't care about looks as much as women think. Women work themselves into a worthless frenzy believing their man wants to fuck every hot chick he sees, including the ones on television. Chill out ladies, even if he wanted to, he couldn't.

The key to not getting screwed is to scrutinize his dick before opening your legs. Fact. Women are equipped to enjoy sex longer and have more orgasms than men. Most importantly, we don't have to get or maintain an erection to have intercourse. When have you ever seen a flaccid penis blast off a nut like a rocket? Limp dicks don't cum. Hard dicks are usually one and done. Maybe two with a recovery period. Vaginas don't require down time. Dicks do.

Women have seven secretion points. Two Skene's and two Bartholin's glands. The Skene's glands aid in a woman's ability to squirt (ejaculate from the urethra) and the Bartholin's release fluids (lubrication) that gets the woman's pussy wet so a man can more easily penetrate her.

Vaginal dryness (outside of medical reasons) happens because men are lazy fuckers. They skip foreplay. They don't care if the woman is aroused or if she has an orgasm. Men nowadays don't understand the complexities of the female anatomy, nor do they care to learn. A woman has to teach a man how to please her. But she must first know how to satisfy herself.

Three female secretion points are *orgasmic*—clitoris, urethra, vagina. Women are a triple threat in the bedroom. Men have only one place to cum from, their urethra. That's it ladies! We have three sexual penetration stations—mouth, vagina and anus. Men have two; their mouth and anus. Pleasure can be derived from each point of entry for both women and men.

I'm writing this book not to degrade men, but to enlighten women.

Ladies, you need to quickly identify men that only want to ejaculate inside of you. Understanding the guys that don't care about you before you have sex with them may save you from being disappointed over and over. When dating, keep your thinking cap on at all times and choose your dick wisely before spreading your legs.

Why don't women get the men they want?

Remember these three things ladies. One, always know what you want from a man. Two, believe that you deserve to be treated like a queen. And three, never be afraid to tell a man what you want (in and out of bed).

Dicks are Dumb

Men are many things, but mind readers they are not.

Know upfront whether you want instant, temporary, or permanent gratification from a guy. If you don't know what you want, he will kindly fuck you and quickly move on to the next woman before you figure it, and him, out.

I'll share some of *my* proven techniques on getting your top-5 team together. I'll also tell you how to keep your star players in rotation and have these guys excited about you! I hear some of you saying, "Top, what? Five?" Stay open-minded ladies. It's hard to get the right dick with that date one at a time bullshit.

Single men are not serial monogamous daters and women shouldn't be either. Ladies, get off the couch and out the house (or date online). You can choose not to bed any of the guys you're vetting until one of them proves worthy, or you can be intimate with as many as you'd like.

There are some guys I've dated for months (or years) and never had sex with them. When you maximize your dickatunities, you actually increase your options in the dating market to find a husband, a lover, a friend with special benefits and/or your best buddy.

Don't be fooled by the myth that men and women can't be friends. Yes, you can have platonic male besties, and don't stop being their friend when you meet a man you're interested in dating.

Most men are fairly intelligent. It's their dick that don't have a brain. I have yet to meet a man that hasn't admitted he's had a dumb dick moment. I write to educate and empower ladies. At the same time, I don't male bash in any of my written works or on my social media pages. I'm unapologetically pro-female. Not anti-male.

If you follow me online, you already know I'm all about my gurlz. Stop settling for nonsense. Fuck these double-standards "don't bring shit to the table but dick" dudes. I honestly don't give a fuck if a man deems me worthy of his time and money. I do the choosing. Not him. What one man won't do, another man will gladly do. Any man that wants to date me, will respect me, do as I ask, or get the hell outta the way of the man who's ready to do the right thing. All women should feel the same.

#HoneyBHonest: Whenever you let a dick choose you, you will get fucked.

When I hear about books like, *He's Just Not That in to You* and *Act Like a Lady, Think Like a Man,* I'm not completely impressed. I respect the authors for their motivation to give us their opinion, but I'm getting ready to connect with women on a deeper level.

It's a fact—when men pen relationship books for women, those men make money. Men know that there are millions of single and lonely (some desperate) women with low self-esteem who have never been married and fear they may never become a bride. I'm not confused why women wholeheartedly believe that men who have cheated on their woman and/or wife are the best men to accept advice from. Some women have been taught they are worthless without a man or husband.

Wait, I'm trying not to jump ahead of myself because there's so much I need to share in this book. So, let me slow down.

Guys bank on, I mean they literally make money off of women that don't use common sense. I hope that's not you, but lots of potential bachelorettes can't comprehend why he won't put a ring on it.

I'll expand on that later.

Having a healthy relationship isn't complicated when women stop wasting time trying to impress the narcissists. Men are more focused on satisfying their dick than pleasing a woman. I have to mention, when I say men, of course I'm not referring to every single man on earth.

Ladies, guys will make you jump through hoops and perform one circus act after another to impress them, then they'll commit to the chick that's a bitch. Don't hate the bitch. She knows what she wants and she knows how to get it.

#HoneyBHonest: Men don't give a fuck about understanding women.

Men have no idea how many women have been sexually damaged before having their first relationship. Or perhaps guys do know because many of them are the ones that have assaulted, battered, molested, or raped young girls and/or women.

When I say young, I'm talking about girls under the age of ten. Fast forward six years, sixteen isn't always so sweet. Lots of females never talk about how they have been sexual abused and mentally scared, often by family members, trusted friends, or their mother's man.

I wish there were legal ramifications for sexual assault such as castration or a male chastity belt (that would function similar to a house arrest bracelet). Men do not hesitate to fuck over women because many of them get away with it.

Thinking about unsolicited sexual advances reminds me of the pastors, with an 's', that tried to seduce me when I was a young girl. The first one was like a father to me. I was about thirteen. I lived a half of a block down the street from him. It was the weekend and I'd decided to visit my best friend, his daughter. The way their shotgun house was designed, I had to go through his bedroom, in order to get to my friend's bedroom. When I entered his bedroom, he locked the door, kissed me on the lips, then said, "I want you to be my spuggie." His pet name indicated I'd be his sexual plaything. The Reverend's wife (whom was in the kitchen at that time) treated me like one of her own children. I exited the front door immediately and didn't go back to my girlfriend's house for over a year.

Another time, one of the reverends at my church invited me to an out-of-town picnic. We stopped by one of my girlfriend's house to pick her up. Her mother let us in, then her mom went toward the back of the (shotgun) house. While sitting in the living room waiting for my girlfriend, the Reverend opened his leather pouch, aligned two rows of cocaine, then sniffed one at a time. Suddenly, I realized why this man always had a runny nose when preaching in the pulpit. I was speechless. At the backyard barbecue, he whisked me off to a bedroom in the house, tried to remove my clothes, and have sex with me. I was fourteen but I was glad I'd invited a nosy girlfriend that rescued me. I can't imagine what would've happened if I hadn't invited her. After that incident, I'd sit in the pew on Sundays and watch this same man tell the congregation fornication was a sin.

What these two pastors didn't realize was that my ninety-two-year-old great-grandfather had beaten both of them to my pussy. At seven years old, I'd already been repeatedly molested. At sixteen, I was sexually assaulted by a stranger on the streets of my hometown in New Orleans. At eighteen, a police officer in New Orleans raped me, then told me, "What are you going to do? Call the police?" He thought nothing of the incident that I've never forgotten. With the exception of the stranger, all of these men were people I'd trusted.

What men, who write books giving women advice on how to find a good man don't understand is, the majority of women have at least one story she could tell about her experience of sexual abuse. There are some girls/women who have been raped repeatedly in foster homes or their own house.

Dicks are Dumb

When I say, "dicks are dumb," it's a fact.

Men do not acknowledge their roles in why some women are sexually repressed while others are promiscuous. Or why some women have a gold-digging, "I'm going to use that motherfucker before he uses me," attitude.

Guys claim they're looking for the right one *while* bragging about having been with a hundred and one. They want a lady after treating other women like whores. I wrote this book because I'm tired of womanizers giving advice to women about relationships and how it's her fault she doesn't have a man.

Most men don't try to understand women. The second they see an attractive female, they think, *I'd love to fuck the shit out of her*. I believe a man will never treat his woman/wife the way he expects another man to respect his daughter. Men that say, "I wish a man would mistreat or disrespect my daughter, I'll shoot his ass," might as well point the gun at himself and pull the trigger if he's the same guy that has intentionally used someone else's baby girl.

Men want us to accept their double standards. Men that use women, abuse women, recklessly sex women raw, abandon women they've impregnated, and secretly despise women wake up and say, "I can tell women how to get a good man because all the doggish shit that shouldn't be done to a woman, I've done those things and more. But I'm a good dog now."

What the fuck ever man, with your bitch ass! Give me a break. I'm getting ready to give it to women straight. What you ladies do with this information is up to you.

Whether he lies through his teeth or bites you on the ass ladies, my point is he's still got the same teeth. Men who have misused countless women in numerous ways, after they tire of doing wrong and can't maintain an erection, want to settle down and get a built-in caretaker—aka wife—that loves them. Men know women are desperate and lots of ladies will accept damn near anything, including being abused for the sake of having a man.

The same sorry ass men that couldn't count their one-night stands on the legs of a centipede are calling women whores. Men who repeatedly fuck women, come inside of women, show up at a woman's front—and, perhaps, back—door at two in the morning feel the woman is not worthy of being his wife because she let him fuck *her* too soon, so she must be that way with every man. In fact, she may be at the bottom of his list of women to fuck, but he doesn't have the balls to tell her the truth because he's preoccupied with busting his next nut and any pussy will do, including hers.

Ladies, I'm here to tell you that women rule. Men know that. They just hope women don't ban together and collectively start owning their power and holding men accountable for their actions.

Dicks are dumb.

How dumb are they? You can start at the top with a former and current President then work your way to the head of the CIA or watch 'em perform on stage, or act on television, or listen to them preach behind the pulpit. Sift through the NFL, NBA, MLB, PGA, or the penitentiary, and sex abusers will stack up higher than the Burj Khalifa. American, German, French, African, Muslim, Indian—every nationality on earth have a long list of dumb as dicks. Female circumcision is horrid but it's still happening in some countries because men don't want women to experience sexual pleasure.

Read this book, a book written by a woman that understands men. I've been married, engaged (gave the ring back), in great relationships (and some fucked up situations). I could be married today to a doctor, politician, baller, blue or white-collar man if I wanted. I have men that love me more than I will ever love them. That's how life should be for every woman, even if she chooses monogamy. I freelance, and have been told that I date like a dude. I consider that a compliment.

If you're looking for a smart dick, you have to search above, below, and in between his heads to find out if he truly gives a fuck about you. Learn what's important to him then capitalize on his emotions. I'll come back to this later in the book, but I want you to zero in on his feelings, ladies.

A dumb dick is easy to spot because it hides behind a set of balls. All he wants to do is fuck you and he'll say whatever dumb shit is necessary to get your goods. Yet, as soon as he pulls out, he's out. Literally.

The smart man is thoughtful. He actually respects you before he beds you and he wants to talk with you the next day and the days after. A wise man plans dates and builds a meaningful relationship with you.

#HoneyBHonest: A dumb dick cums every chance it gets.

A hole is a hole is a hole even if it's an asshole. Ladies, it's up to you to interview the dick. It's not the kind of Q&A the dick is praying for. Trust me.

Training a dick is like learning to speak a foreign language. It will not happen overnight. First you must be able to identify what kind of dick you have. I'm not going to lie; it's hard, but I'm willing to help you if you accept that you cannot convert a cheater.

You'll have to do a background check on his dick to find out where it's been, what it's been up and in to. Also, what has this dick done for the women he came inside of before meeting you? If he brags about all the things he's done for other women, do not accept less from him. A man does not get credit for storytelling.

Ladies have to think ahead of the dick. You'll have to develop a strategic plan to test his DIQ. You'll have to know what the dick is thinking before the dick knows what it's thinking. Look him in his eyes. This part isn't as hard as it seems when you ask (his dick) the right questions.

Dicks do not roll over or do what you want them to simply because you scream, cry, or call yourself dicktating his whereabouts. Training the one you like will require a great degree of patience and persistence.

Lastly, you'll have to administer a pass or fail challenge. If he's close, you decide if you want to grade his dick on a curve. If he fails, do not keep giving him chances. Let that dumb ass dick go.

It's time for women to exercise their female power and stop shrinking. No more being brainwashed by dicks that only want to use your good pussy as a sperm bank. No more catering to a man hoping and praying he likes you or that he won't leave you.

If you want to keep getting what you're getting, put my book down. If you want to learn more about men, and yourself, keep turning the pages.

When you think about it ladies, dicks like brain (fellatio); they do not have one. Dicks are incapable of processing information. They don't remember shit. So exactly how are you going to conquer this arduous task? Not by acting like a lady or thinking like a man.

Ladies, you have to learn when to act like a bitch and how to think like a dick.

I

Women Must Think for Themselves

1
A Woman's Worth

Know thyself. Don't be afraid to be a boss bitch. Be your best. Do your best. Then you must expect the best from yourself and others in your life.

Start this chapter by asking yourself a simple, yet powerful question.

"Who am I?"

Don't rush your response. This is one of the most important chapters in the book. *A Woman's Worth* is number one because too many women devalue themselves. You have got to stop allowing men to define you.

I want you to say aloud, "I am worthy. I am brilliant. I am powerful. I am sexy. I am hurting. I am too giving. I am grieving. I am healing. I am lonely. I give more to others than I invest in myself. I am confident. I am angry. I am happy. Dammit I'm tired of putting everyone else first! It's my time to shine."

#HoneyBHonest: Women are complex, not complicated.

Whatever is in your heart at this moment, speak *your* truth without hesitation. Say it aloud. Hear yourself. Listen to yourself. Then ask yourself, why am I brilliant? What makes me powerful? Why do I give too much to others? What do I care about the most? What do I want to do with *my* life? Is this how I want to live?

Give each of your questions and answers serious thought then document your response. My recommendation is that you start a daily journal with a voice memo, record a video, place notes in your phone, or create a file on your computer. If you prefer, write it down.

It's easy to rise to low expectations when you don't know your self-worth.

HoneyBHonest: There is no right or wrong answer. Do you have high or low self-esteem? Maybe you're like most females, somewhere in between, wishing you had more confidence, especially when dealing with men. After reading *Dicks Are Dumb* you'll view men differently. More importantly, you'll see yourself in a new light. Others will notice the change within you without you having to speak a word.

Remember this, boss bitches exude attitude.

Now, I want you to do an exercise. Begin your affirmations with the words, "I deserve" and, "I want". This may seem elementary or tedious, but I find that most women don't know what they want, and if they do, they don't believe they're deserving of the love and relationship they desire. Too many women are attracting and settling for mediocre men. Some women are celibate because they're fed up, holding out, or have given up on finding a man who genuinely loves them.

Knowing yourself and what you want immediately increases your self-worth. Let this moment be all about you. Be present with yourself.

Some of your responses to, "Who am I"? "I deserve", "I want", are rooted in the mistakes you've made along the way. You might feel guilty about having let men take advantage of you. Or embarrassed due to sexual assault or molestation. Don't blame yourself. Seriously. I care about what you've done and been through, but you are alive for a reason and your change starts now. If you're holding on to guilt, forgive yourself this very second.

It might be something small like you cursed a dude out, now you're feeling bad. Nah, fuck him! You cursed his sorry ass out for a reason. Don't beat yourself up fearing he won't communicate with you. He probably will, because men like bitches. It's true. I want you to use positive energy to better yourself.

No one is perfect. Every woman has challenges that men cannot relate to. When you cry, one of two things happen: men either want to fix the problem or they don't care why you're upset. Either way, most men won't give you the attention you need at that time. He wants you to shut up and/or go away.

Women must stop being invisible.

All the things you've done are embedded in the blueprint of your life. Do not accept any man's judgment of you. Tell him, "I'm not your fucking problem." You can stop there, or add, "I'm not co-signing on your bullshit. Look in the mirror and handle that motherfucker. When you see a real man, you let me know."

Lots of men have extremely low self-esteem so they stand on your shoulders with both feet and weigh you down. They curse you. Make you believe you're nothing without them. They get inside your head by degrading you.

I want you to use your experiences, good and bad, to create your masterpiece of worthiness. Take every negative comment a man has told you. Write it on a piece of paper. Stick it on a poster board. Then one-by-one, cover those negative phrases with positive ones until you no longer see the hurt. Repeat, believe, embrace all things positive into your heart and mind.

Dicks are Dumb

If a man ever attempts to put you down again, calmly let him know—verbally, via text, or direct message, "I love me more than I love you."

The new you will have haters and naysayers who will not support you through your transformation. Give them (men and women) a good reason to be jealous. Without saying, make them wish they were you. Smile often. You are doing better than you may think you are.

Note: You are unique. You are special. You are fabulous! Believe that.

Think about how you were reared. From religion to sex, the 'dos' and the 'don'ts' of your childhood influences the woman you are today. But that woman may not be the person trapped inside of you dying to get out.

You've got to let your inner star shine.

All your life people may have told you what you should be. How you should act. What you should think, say, and feel. They critique everything from your hair to your shoes and everything in between. Friends want to tell you whether you should keep or leave *your* man. Your man wants you to cook, clean, work, and suck his dick.

Who cares about what you want?

Starting now, you do! Out with the old you right this second. Love yourself so much that your decision to let others enter your space is crystal clear, absent of all doubt.

The degree to which your upbringing dictates who you are today depends on how much you allow the past to influence your presence. How do you view your life in this moment? Your outlook is rooted in the good and bad things that happened to you. Bad things happen to good women and innocent little girls. If bad things have happened to you, is not your fault.

Let's focus on where you are now. What are your personal and professional goals? What do you dream your life to become in the next weeks, months, years? You can have that. The only person that has the power to deny your happiness is you.

A man cannot define you without your permission. Being in or out of a rela–that's short for relationship–does not determine your self-worth. Your parents or guardians instilled their values in you, but you cannot live your life for them. Stop trying to please everybody. Know what matters most to you and why.

HoneyBHonest: If a man is not on your page, end the chapter, and start anew.

Your book. Your life. Your story. Write it. Live it. Show it through the lens of your soul.

For those of you saying, "I want what my parents had," stop. You can never have what your parents had because the truth is you don't know what they had. You only saw what they showed you, but there's always more to a rela than what people witness.

Know what *you* want.

Going back to your conception you had things that couldn't be taught like personality and talent. Maybe you were funny, introverted, or extroverted. Someone all the others followed. Or you were an artist forever creating things. Perhaps you enjoyed singing and were good at it. You may have been a dancer, comedian, a politician in the making, or the greatest debater in your class. Multiple characteristics were inside of you while you were inside of your mother's womb.

As a kid, no one had to teach you the right way to sing your first song, how to dance, or what to say in order to make people laugh. You discovered your gifts out of one thing—love. The day someone told you that you weren't good enough, or what you'd never become, made you do one of two things: believe your parents were right, or try to prove them wrong. Sad, but true, most females are followers with leadership capabilities. If for no one but yourself, know that you are in charge of your life.

Other people's voices are embedded in your subconscious. It's time to give yourself permission not to listen to those people in your head anymore. It's time for you to embrace the loving little girl inside of you. Imagine her. Hold her. Heal her. Love her. Let her sing, dance, and be happy.

What are your gifts?

Yes, you have more than one. It's okay if you're unsure of what they are. Start by following your passion. My ability to write was in the words I penned before I realized I'd become a *New York Times* bestselling author. That list was reserved for intelligent white authors.

I was a fairly smart teenager, but I was clueless when it came to my career goals. I was terrified knowing that I had none. I wondered, how was I going to support myself after I graduated. Never had I dreamt of becoming a *New York Times* best-selling author. In the ninth grade (at McDonogh 35 Senior High), I wrote an essay entitled, *We Were Born to Die*, and my teacher loved it! Since 1978, his praise made me want to impress everyone with my words.

I worked for the federal government from the age of eighteen until I retired at thirty-five. Communicating was my job and I took my responsibilities seriously. My memos evoked feelings the readers could not ignore. I recall my supervisor telling me to take out the emotions.

Timing matters when taking a leap of faith but it's never going to be impeccable. Society is constantly desensitizing and discouraging us. Always *tell us* what not to do, where not to go. *Don't resign from your job or divorce your husband. Don't relocate to a different city or country.* This is not to suggest you don't have supporters in your life, but unfortunately, you begin to embody the fears of those giving you their opinion.

Whenever someone tells me, "You should write this story," I say, "A writer without an idea for book needs to get a job." Or I respond, "That's your life. Write it yourself."

Often, we remember insults faster than a compliment.

My last supervisor did me a huge favor. Prior to his saying tone it down, I hadn't realized how excited I was about writing, but I knew I wanted to make the reader feel–good, bad– anything! Just feel me dammit!

What sparked my decision to resign from a nearly six-figure position back in 1999? According to my boss, my performance was stellar. The time had come for my promotion to his grade level, GS-15. I requested my salary increase, private office, and reserved parking space. Instantly, he advised me I wasn't doing well. I needed to be on a productivity improvement plan, and I had to write my own PIP.

Immediately, I stopped working at 5;00pm. I no longer stayed until 8:00pm to prepare the talking notes for his meetings. At the end of each work day, when he was on the elevator, I stood beside him. I began writing every night.

Outraged that he could no longer articulate complete statistical data to his superiors, he called me in to his office. Told me I was a disappointment. Said, I let him down. When he was done talking, my response was, "You can't have it both ways. You either pay me what I'm worth, or you get what you're paying for. Right now, you are getting what you're paying for."

His face turned beet red. I did not care that he re-assigned me to report to the black woman. She got what they were paying for too. For the first time in my career, I was my own boss.

What motivates you?

What do people praise you for? Cooking? Interior design? Coordinating events? Do you like tending to children or the elderly? Can you start up corporations? Are you popular on social media? Do you have the gift of gab that makes people eager to hear your opinion? Maybe you've put off writing your book. Many people think they have everyone else figured out. Have you ever taken time to figure out yourself?

My moment of courage came in 1993, on the last day of class at Berkeley Community College. Our English teacher asked each of her students to share what we'd planned to do after graduation. I stood and said, "I'm going to write a book, and the title is, *Soulmates Dissipate*." If you haven't read this novel, please download or buy it now.

Seven years later, June of 2000, I self-published *Soulmates Dissipate*. I'd heard Oprah say, "If you sell ten thousand copies of a self-published novel, you'll get a book deal." September 2000, Kensington Publishing Corporation offered and I accepted a three-book deal.

Whatever you want to do, go for it!

I drew down my retirement, less than $15,000, invested every penny into my book, and borrowed a total of $3,000 ($500 each) from my mother-figure, sister, ex-boyfriend, and three friends. I had eleven thousand and four copies of *Soulmates Dissipate* delivered to my front door and stored them in my garage. In less than ninety days, with the support of family, friends, bookstores, distributors, book clubs, and some of you reading this, almost every copy was sold!

Did I ever want to give up? Yes. For about three hours, I had a pity party. I told myself all the reasons why people wouldn't buy this shit. Told myself, "I wouldn't buy this shit."

What was really happening was a breakthrough. I was afraid of failure. At the same time, I feared success. I didn't want to believe that God had blessed me with the talent to write. I was no journalism major. Nor did I have a four-year college degree.

As a young shy black girl, I grew up in New Orleans, Louisiana wearing hand-me-downs from the white family my great-aunt (who was my guardian) worked for. I hated most of the clothes that were passed on to me by a teenage white girl.

Who inspires you? Who encourages you to be your best and value your worth? It's not always those closest to us. In fact, often the people who see our talent, are strangers. God gives us everything we need to succeed. Man gives us every reason to fail.

Whether you speak to someone, talk to yourself aloud, or regurgitate negativity in your mind, what you tell yourself is powerful. Filter goodness into your spirit. Find your source of strength.

I have tremendous faith. Not in myself, but in God. All I have to do is put in the work. You do too! Don't overthink your worthiness. Just know it exists. Don't allow anyone to put you down. I boldly tell people, "Don't waste your life trying to live mine." No one can breathe for you so no one can live for you.

Are you the woman that constantly gives to others but has a hard time receiving presents and compliments? If someone says, "You look beautiful." Do you think or respond with, "Thanks, but I need to lose weight." If your answer is, "Yes," you need to stop and focus on loving yourself.

Now if you're that woman who feels the world is indebted to you and you take all that you can with little to no consideration of how much others sacrifice for you, you have unresolved issues that most likely stem from your childhood.

Giving and taking too much are both signs of low self-esteem. If you give all the time, you don't believe you are worthy of praise. When you take all the time, you don't give a fuck about anyone except yourself. In order to know your worth, you must first understand how to balance your life. Learn when and how to give and receive, especially in a relationship.

Does having a man come before your happiness? Do you put your man before your parents, children, family, and friends when you know he's not worthy? Do you constantly find fault with your body image? Do you invest time—

your most valuable asset—in others before you do in yourself?

If you answered "yes" to any of these questions, you have a lot of growing to do.

You deserve the best! Act like it and others will respond in kind. From this second forward, make your mental, physical, spiritual, and financial stability your primary investment. Those who don't respect you will distance themselves from you because they see you're elevating and outgrowing them. It's okay to let some people go. Maybe temporarily. Perhaps permanently.

I wholeheartedly love myself, my family, my friends, my fans, and I love men too. It's my energy and personality that allows men to feel comfortable and fall for my boss bitch attitude. My knowledge of what turns a man on in and out of the bedroom keeps men more interested in me, than I am in them.

Don't forget the title of this book ladies. It's true.

I'll share a few of my sexual secrets with you later in the book.

There are many reasons why not enough women have great self-esteem. In part, it's a generational mentality and gross misunderstanding of what being a woman truly means. Have you defined womanhood for yourself? Being strong is not the same as having high self-esteem.

HoneyBHonest: Because a woman does it all doesn't mean she has it all together.

Know what you want and believe you deserve the best. Then you need to have tremendous faith in whatever higher power you believe in. Don't be afraid to express yourself. Stop giving a fuck about what men think of you. You'll see after you change your approach to how you deal with men that a lot of them are extremely needy. Be bold, but understand that you don't have to be boisterous to get what you want.

Hey, ladies. I couldn't leave this out. The next chapter goes into detail. To know your worth means you must fall in love with your pussy. I'm seriously concerned that some women are uncomfortable saying the word pussy. Others have a serious disconnect with their vagina. That's not right.

True Story: A guy interested in dating me said, "You think you're all that."

My response was, "No, you think I'm all that. I know I'm all that. Whatever your feelings are toward me is a reflection of your low self-esteem. Let's do us a favor. Don't ever call me again in your life." I haven't spoken with or seen that guy since and that was over fifteen years ago.

If you detect a man has abusive tendencies, disassociate yourself immediately. Don't justify his madness. Men want to fuck you, then they don't want to fuck with you. Know what you want and get it upfront. Otherwise, let him bust that nut in the palm of his hand. Knowing your self-worth allows you to walk away from men who aren't worthy of your greatness.

Ladies—one day at a time, one dude at a time, one dick at a time—you got this!

Recommended Reading: *Sweeter than Honey* by Mary B. Morrison

2
Value Your Vagina

Most women don't have a relationship with their pussy. Men want to keep it that way. I hope to inspire women to develop a connection with their vagina. Anything that isn't valued is easily given away.

There is power in your pussy. Yassss ma'am. Your vulva is amazing!

Did your mother tell you, or have you taught your daughter that women have seven secretion points? I've explained each one earlier in this book and will touch on the matter again in this section. Most men are clueless and some, if they haven't read this book, believe women have only one. The ignorance men possess regarding women and what's between a woman's thighs, is largely in part why men should not write relationship books for women. I'm tired of men telling women what we need to do to get and keep a man satisfied when most men are liars and cheaters, including the self-proclaimed good men.

HoneyBHonest: One cannot appreciate what one does not understand.

There are women who think they urinate from their vagina. Some females believe they have one secretion point, maybe two. Actually, three of your seven secretion points—clitoris, vagina, urethra—are highly orgasmic and can bring you tremendous pleasure.

Love is not all a woman needs, but good loving sure does improve a woman's self-esteem. I have lots of knowledge about sex and relationships but I'm not clinically trained, board certified, nor do I have a degree in psychology. I read nonfiction books on various subject matters and have analyzed male and female behavior for over thirty-five years. I discovered Ben-Wa balls, adult toys, experienced my first orgasm, and a lot more in my teens.

I'm a relationship sexpert, and the creator and instructor of my *Vaginal Aerobics, Head Master,* and *Date Like a Mistress* (especially if you have a man) classes. I teach women and men how to embrace intimacy with themselves and one another. With my life-skill credentials in mind, I'll share what I know about the vagina.

Many women experience their first orgasm from external stimulation of the clitoris, which has six to eight thousand nerve endings in what's sometimes referred to as 'the pearl.' Your pearl is located outside of your vagina; therefore, no penetration is necessary in order to climax. You probably didn't have your first orgasm prior to losing your virginity, but if you knew then what you're reading now, you could have pleasured yourself before the painful tearing of your hymen.

Are you aware that a man's foreskin is to his virginity as the hymen is to ours? Yes, the detachment of the foreskin from the corona hurts like hell but it was God's way of having both man and woman exchange pain (before pleasure) while mating for the first time.

Adolescent males could not readily enjoy masturbation if they were uncircumcised. Men discovered a medical procedure—

circumcision—that is now performed immediately after birth to ensure boys would never have to endure excruciating pain during any form of friction.

Believe me when I tell you, dicks are dumb, and men are selfish as fuck!

God did not make a mistake. Foreskin is purposeful and so is the hymen, but why isn't there a procedure to remove hymen tissue at birth for girls? Female genital mutilation/circumcision is the removal of the external genitalia. Some countries perform that procedure on females as a standard practice. What the fuck?! Men, those egotistical bastards remove the clitoris to prevent women from enjoying sex prior to penetration, and to minimize a woman's ability to do so in less than sixty seconds. Yes, women can cum in less than a minute from clitoral stimulation. The hymen isn't removed because men derive pleasure from using their dick to one, inflict sexual pain on women; and two, men need a way of proving their dick was her first.

Your pussy is so powerful that men use and abuse it to control you. Too many women freely allow men to fuck and fuck over them. Wake up ladies! Stop allowing men to set an agenda for your pussy.

Under educating, miseducation, and simply not talking to girls about the complexities of their bodies is a major disservice to females everywhere. Women must stop relying on men to give them sexual satisfaction.

The average dick couldn't care less whether you cum or not. Some women have given birth and have never had the pleasure of a single orgasm. Others can climax from oral copulation but not penetration. This could be due to sexual trauma or from having horribly selfish lovers. In most instances, men do not care if a woman is sexually satisfied.

I say, "Stab his ass in the middle of his heads with a rubber fork." You're not trying to hurt him, but you will get his attention. Okay, don't do that. But you get my point. You need to be a boss bitch when it comes to valuing your vagina.

HoneyBHonest: Get yours first!

Climaxing for the first time from vaginal penetration can come as a surprise or be difficult, if you let a man have complete control. If he's moving too fast, tell him to slow down. If he's too slow, you speed up to a pace to your liking by moving your hips. Getting on top puts you in a position of power. Some women are reluctant to ride a man's dick and/or his face. Don't be. If you fall over, get back up and on top of him! There are plenty of comfortable positions where you can intertwine your body with his, caress one another, be present in the moment and make love all night or as long as you'd like. It's your pussy. Learn how to please yourself.

HoneyBHonest: Any man that complains about your pussy is a bitch.

Did you know that the vagina has pockets/crevices like a pool table? Left corner might be your . . . jackpot! Or penile pressure applied to the right side may make you cum hard. When balls are racked on a table, consider the odd numbered balls in that triangle hot spots inside your womb. If a man's stroke is weak, angle is off, or he's not focused on you, he cannot properly navigate his penis around your vagina, nor will he give you enough strong strokes to fill your G-Spot with ejaculate fluids. Most men don't know their average stroke count prior to cumming.

Every woman does not squirt like a water fountain. Some gush like a waterfall. Unless a woman has an impeding medical reason, every woman has the ability to squirt (some in under a minute) but only one out of ten do so. Here's why you may not have experienced the pleasure of squirting. If you've ever had the urination sensation during sex, and chose to be lady-like, stopped, and used the restroom to empty your bladder, there's a strong possibility you were on the verge of squirting. Instead, you flushed all that good ejaculate fluid down the toilet. The pre-squirting sensation drives a lot of women insane. They don't understand what's happening to their body. From head to toes, women feel as though they're about to lose control. Next time, keep going. Relax and push until you gush!

Did you know that the bladder cuts itself off (for men and women) during sex? The fluids that build up in the G-Spot during intercourse are clear and odorless. Female ejaculation has two helpers called Skene's glands, which are located on opposite sides of your urethra. Just as a man cums and urinates from his urethra, a woman squirts and urinates from her urethra.

I'd be remiss not to let you know that the purpose of precum is to cleanse bacteria from the male's urethra prior to ejaculation to minimize infecting his sperm. Precum can lubricate but that's not its purpose. Ok, I'm not sure what you're going to do with that information, but now you know you might not want to swallow or lap up his precum.

I'm going back to the Bartholin's glands. You have two pinholes aka secretion points at the base entry of your vagina (one on each side). The purpose of these glands is to get the pussy wet. When a man excites a woman, the vagina self-lubricates for his entry. The problem nowadays is most men want to bypass touching, teasing, and turning on a woman, and get straight to fucking. They rub a woman's precious body all rough and shit, and at the same time he's grabbing his dick, then forcing it inside of her vagina. If the woman is dry, he blames her but it's his damn fault. If a woman medically has vaginal dryness, inserting a little coconut oil prior to penetration helps her enjoy sex.

There's no roadmap to intimacy. Do it your way, not his, ladies. You'll feel better. Women deserve to be aroused before a dumb ass man goes stuffing his dick in the pussy.

HoneyBHonest: It's a woman's responsibility to value her vagina.

Never accept a man telling you, your pussy is no good. I mean never! A man's verbal attack of the vagina (or the woman) is his way of expressing his sexual inadequacy. His issues may range from erectile dickfunction to impotence. Weak ass men are assholes. Degrading women make men feel better about themselves and their dick.

HoneyBHonest: Men care more about their dick than they do about their woman.

You don't have to agree with me, but if a man's dick stops getting hard, or he has to take male enhancements to perform, or he can't keep up with your sex drive, or you allow another man to penetrate you (for whatever reason), your man will lose his fucking mind. Just remember it's not about you, it's about his dick. Men cheat all the time but cannot handle the thought, let alone the act, of another man's dick inside of his woman. Relax, ladies, you'll never win his argument because it's not about you.

Question— Now that you better understand the power your vagina possesses, why would you grant access to any man that is not worthy? You've got the main thing men want and he'll do practically anything to release himself inside of you. Sure, he could and probably does jackoff, even if he's married, but there's nothing like the real thing ladies, and you've got the goods.

Men crave cumming in a nice, tight, cushy, warm place. They know there are women willing to grant access with little to no forethought. Men cheat because they want to cum inside of a new—not better pussy. Unless they are working, men think about sex all day. What did I say earlier? After he cums, he's out. Literally. Remember dicks are dumb before you let a man fuck you.

HoneyBHonest: A woman's ass should never be wetter than her wallet.

Can you count how many times a man has ejaculated inside of you? I know some of you know exactly how many men you've dated, but that's not what I asked. Have you heard of, or ever had, a vaginal cleanse? You can Google V-Tox, vaginal steam, or vaginal detox to find a location in your area. I recommend every woman have one.

You sit on a chair, draped in a plastic cape, naked underneath for thirty to sixty minutes. The chair has an opening that allows the steam to rise up and cleanse/detox your womb. The steam pot beneath your hips (kind of like a crockpot) is filled with lots of (tea like) herbs that are healthy for the vagina. In addition to cleansing, the steam may aide in reducing heavy bleeding, decreasing menstrual pain, tightening your vaginal walls, and more.

I feel exhilarated and spiritually uplifted each time I detox my vagina. The frequency is up to you but every now and then, women need to rid their uterus of a man's energy, which is sometimes toxic within itself, especially after a divorce or bad breakup.

A lot of women, myself included, were never taught to value themselves, their virginity, or their vagina. Some of you, like me, figured it out along the way. I allowed a teenage boy (age sixteen) access to my virginity when I was fourteen. As a result, I became impregnated, and miscarried. I'd never known which would've been worse, losing my baby or giving birth. I remember being hospitalized, and feeling like I was going to die!

Fast forward, I married the same guy at twenty-one. I had a baby with him at twenty-two. We separated when I was twenty-three (my decision) because he'd fractured my nose, blackened my eye to the point I couldn't open it, busted my lip, and I had to have my brow stitched back together.

Praise God, I knew my worth. I got the hell out of that marriage immediately. He apologized, cried, and begged repeatedly for me to take him back. I refused each time. No way in hell was I going to let him penetrate my vagina after beating me. The divorce was final when I was twenty-four, but I'd moved on with dating shortly after the altercation.

Which brings me to this— I'm sick and tired of society trying to put a time on how long divorced or separated women should wait before dating again. Men don't wait. Hell, most men are fucking around while they're in a relationship. Ladies, stop letting men tell you what to do with your pussy.

I don't use the fact that I did not know my body at fourteen, nor never being taught how to love myself as an excuse for the numerous things I've tried sexually. Nor do I feel ashamed for the things I allowed boys and men to do to or with me. I own my choices. And for the men that molested, raped, and abused me, I thank God for granting me the wisdom to accept and understand that none of those things were my fault.

Here are three important reasons why you need to value your vagina:

- Your chichi (pronounced she-she) is yours. She does not belong to anyone else. You are 100% responsible for her overall health. Protect your pussy.

- Shared with the wrong man, your vagina can make you emotionally unstable aka a crazy bitch! Having his baby or sexing him whenever he wants will not make him stay with you. Stop bartering your pussy for peanuts.

- Your vagina is your sanctuary. She can bring you pleasure and boost your confidence when you respect and appreciate her. Pamper your pussy.

Prior to having intercourse for the first time, most women don't truly understand their worth and they aren't confident or comfortable with their body image. Mainly because girls allow the media to set their standard for beauty. I'll expand upon this in the next section.

Please establish a relationship with your vagina. Don't take her for granted or give her away. Every time you have sex, the choice should be clear. The decision is yours. It's a disgrace for any woman to feel guilty of for saying, "No," when she doesn't want to participate in intercourse.

HoneyBHonest: Your pussy. Your prerogative.

Insecurities can lead to you having a hard time saying no to a boy/man that pressures you for sex. Never feel obligated to please a guy fearing he'll move on to another female if you don't have sex with him. Refusing a man usually makes him more interested in you.

Dicks are Dumb

In high school (before my miscarriage), I learned important things about safe sex and vaginal health in my sex education class that proved helpful throughout my life. My teachers taught me how to tell when you may have contracted a sexually transmitted disease. What to do and where to go for free services if you suspect you have an STD. What can happen if a STD goes untreated. That was scary! What a condom looks like, and how and why it's used. What services Planned Parenthood offered.

I knew I was sexually active but I couldn't talk to my guardians about it. I'd gone to Planned Parenthood and received birth control. I was taking the pill until a letter showed up in the mailbox at our home, and my great-aunt cursed me out, and took my pills. Her anger did not keep me from devaluing my vagina. I wasn't having sex because I wanted to. I did it because my boyfriend wanted to. Months later, I was pregnant. I was educated enough to go back on contraceptives and not let my great-aunt find out.

Most girls (and women) are ignorant about their body. Sex education is not an invitation for teens and pre-teens to be promiscuous. Sex education in schools saves lives. Parents who withhold information from and avoid having open conversations with their children, are putting their children at a risk for teen pregnancy, STDs, rape, molestation, and more.

Going to church every Sunday was mandatory, but it didn't take away my curiosity about sex. I was told by my great-aunt, "Don't do it. You're not going to be half the woman your mother was." Well, my mother gave birth to eight children and had one known miscarriage. She married my dad, then ultimately committed suicide when I was nine years old. My father was a chronic physical abuser. My dad taught me (through his actions) what not to accept from men.

Ladies, you should never lay with a man that lay hands on you. No woman deserves to be abused. But I understand how hard it is for some of you to let go of someone you love and maybe have children with. If you stay, don't ask— demand that he never hits you again. If he does, leave. The longer you stay, the harder it becomes to leave a man.

HoneyBHonest: Accepting abuse makes a woman devalue herself and her vagina.

Men lie to, cheat on, and disrespect women, but the second a woman opens her legs for another man, all of sudden, they care. Not about you. He's concerned about his property. His pussy was given away. Somebody has to pay. The other guy might be confronted. His woman may be battered or emotionally degraded, I mean with hardcore words like bitch, whore, or prostitute. He might end the relationship, hate his woman, and never speak to her again.

HoneyBHonest: The pulse of a man's dick is in his asshole . . . ego.

Very few men are taught to respect and appreciate a woman's vagina. Men receive accolades for dogging women out. Ladies, don't allow a man to make your pussy his prized possession. You are a total package.

Exactly how do you learn how to value your vagina?

The first requirement is to love yourself. Believe in yourself. Stop censoring what you have to say to a man when you know all he's interested in is sexing you. I'm not suggesting you be rude to anyone. Humor and sarcasm works well for me. However, if you're not honest with him, the first person you lie to is yourself.

Some women will cook for and have sex with a man before he takes her out. Don't volunteer to be his maid and sex slave, especially if you want him to marry you. If you want to enjoy his company, have great sex, and don't care if you ever see him again, there is nothing wrong with your decisions. I've done that but I don't cook.

Too many ladies start off accommodating the man first, then you want his consideration after you've set his expectations really high without giving him an incentive or a single reason to do anything for you. Give that some thought.

A woman can't train a dog by giving him a treat before he learns to sit, beg, rollover, fetch, and jump. If a lady feels she has to prove herself to a man, she's teaching a man how to play dead, not answer her calls, and ignore her texts.

Ladies, learn how to dangle your pussy in his face like a piñata but don't let him hit it. Licking is okay though. Seriously. Don't share your vagina before a man does what you want him to do. If he doesn't do what you'd like, he wasn't going to do what you wanted anyway. You've lost nothing. Move forward. More importantly, you didn't compromise your vagina and your integrity.

Ladies, be patient when getting to know a man. Let the man set the tone for the relationship. If he's a gentleman, he's going to respect and do for you in the beginning and throughout the rela. If he's all talk and no action, he's a user. Don't think or treat this guy special. He doesn't care where he gets laid.

This next message is for you. Be clear on your intentions before you have sex. Trust me, a man knows what he wants from you and sometimes all he wants is sex. I'm not suggesting you wait for months, or until he puts a ring on your finger but if marriage is what you want, you need a strategy.

Don't be eager to walk down the aisle for the sake of a title. In many instances, marriage is undervalued. So is the vagina. If you don't know your worth, don't expect a man to figure it out. That's not his responsibility. It's yours.

A lot of guys don't mind wining and dining in hopes to get the pussy. Until he shows you he's worth opening your legs for, continue to date other men. Dating and sexing are totally separate. You don't have to bed anyone if you're not interested. However, if sex is all you want, be okay with your decision. Don't expect him to change his mind, if you have a change of heart because the two of you had sex and the dick was great.

Please don't frown here and act like you've never had casual sex. Or think other women are sluts, whores, and whatnot when they do. You have no more power over other women's vagina as they have none over yours. Women who degrade other women aren't happy with themselves. Don't be that woman.

Men who have casual sex are having it with someone. You need to stay focused and understand why you're sharing your vagina (or not).

Valuing your vagina is far more complicated than you imagine. It encompasses a deep comprehension of what you do and why you screw.

Lots of men have no idea if the woman they're with has been sexually abused. I'll discuss more about sex after abuse later in the book.

If you haven't done so, take a picture of your vagina. Get a hand mirror and look at her. Taste yourself. Don't you dare frown. You should never serve what you refuse to eat. What do you taste like? Smell like? Look like? You should know your vagina better than anyone else, including your gynecologist. It's your pussy!

True Story: A guy I dated told me, "If I ever catch my woman having sex with another man, I'm going to make him get on top of her. Then I'm going to shoot him in the back of his head and make sure the bullet goes through him and her and kill both of them at the same time."

Needless to say, he's history.

I share this story to show you how crazy some men are over pussy. He said he would kill them. I believed him. How can all the loving, caring, and sharing moments a man (or woman) has be thrown away in an instance over cheating?

HoneyBHonest: Men often tell women how they really feel but most women aren't great listeners.

Women hear what they want to hear. Some are so tuned-in to what men say about other women that they miss what the man says about them. If you do that, you're setting yourself up for a failed relationship.

Put this book down for a moment and spend some time valuing your vagina!

Recommended Reading:
Who's Loving You by Mary B. Morrison

3
Baby Girls and Baby Dolls

Baby doll love is real. Before a girl learns to spell or write her name, often she's given a doll. She hears, "You're such a good mommy." Subliminally, she's taught her role in society is to cater to something/someone other than herself. She internalizes the praises and develops emotions that are external of loving herself. This little girl may be the child inside of you.

She loves her baby and doesn't realize that she longs to become a good mommy. I'll say this again, "She loves *her* baby." Cradles, hugs, combs hair, changes diapers, bathes, dresses and undresses, rocks and feeds her baby. Perhaps, she's given a dollhouse, stroller, and other items (for her baby) before she can spell her first name.

She's taught and/or shown directly and/or indirectly that women are supposed to have babies when the truth is, every woman does not want to be a mother. But she's gravely influenced starting with the moment she's given her first, her own baby.

Girls are encouraged to be the best caretaker they can be when they're complimented, praised, and adored by family, friends, and strangers who see a toddler or adolescent playing the role of a mother. A little girl's desire may develop prematurely to one day have a real baby she can love, especially if she feels unloved by either or both of her parents.

A few years later, often in the pre-adolescent stage of her life, her doll has breasts bigger than hers along with a flatter stomach, luxurious hair, and long, slender sexy legs. Nine times out of ten her doll looks nothing like her.

She dreams of one day having breasts like the doll. Hair like her doll's. Desiring to be what she is not, her self-esteem diminishes. She's intrigued with what's between her doll's legs even if there's no mock genital. As she grows older, she may get a male doll to court her female doll and now she's romantically dreaming of being a mother, wife, and having a family (of her own) before she gets her period or sees her own vagina. Whatever that is. She probably hasn't had 'the talk' yet. Not the "this is your kitty" talk. It is important for girls to be talked to frankly. I mean the "this is your vagina and here's how it functions" talk. And don't omit explaining hormones. No amount of "don't let a little boy put his thing inside of you" will eradicate God giving children mating tools like pheromones. All animals have procreation instincts, including little girls.

At some point, she'll love a boy the way she loves her baby. And if he gives her an ounce of attention, a hug and a kiss...oh boy! She instantly falls in, what she really knows little about, love. She'll lie about her whereabouts to be with a boy because she feels good, not about herself, about him.

Mama might be single and head of household working extra hours to pay the bills. Daddy may think he's parenting because he's present, when he's actually emotionally detached from his baby girl while she's in her room playing with dolls. Whatever preoccupies his daughter allows him uninterrupted time to text his side chicks, watch porn on his cell, or enjoy a game of sports on television. That's if he resided in the home with his daughter.

Who shows real love to the baby girl before she starts imitating adulthood by having sex with a boy who tells her all the things she's longed to hear? You're beautiful. You're so fine. I like you. Be my girlfriend. Let's have sex. You're a virgin, you can't get pregnant. You can trust me.

If a little girl is fortunate to have both parents show her love, the baby doll has pre-programed her for motherhood and she's ready to be with the boy that is full of empty promises. She believes in him more than her parents. She's in love but not with herself. From birth to birthing babies, women love men that don't love them.

This can change. The first thing adults need to do is leave the baby dolls on the shelves at the department stores, especially if abortion in America becomes illegal. Before a little girl starts talking, take the time to observe and learn what she's interested in. No one probably did this for you at a very early age, but promoting self-love and not gifting baby dolls before she knows herself can help build your daughter's self-esteem. If she asks for a doll, ask why does she want one. Then explain to her babies cost time and money.

Explain to her, "You don't have a job. You don't want your baby to be on welfare. You'll need a good father to support you and the baby. When you graduate from college, own a business or get a full-time job with benefits, and have a husband, then you can have a baby doll, but don't give it to my grandchild." What you're doing is teaching her to make informative and conscious decisions in an orderly manner. She'll eventually comprehend if a guy is not going to marry her, or if he's broke, she's not having his baby.

Boys are given action figures, guns, and most boys enjoy playing video games (some extremely violent). While girls are being taught to be sensitive, boys are being desensitized and destructive. Let's move forward.

A Teenage Girl Gets Her Period
The talk, if it happens at all, is far too often overly censored. There is little to no discussion regarding how a girl connects with and values her vagina. Teaching her the importance and purpose of her vagina should be introduced years before she starts menstruating. Some girls' cycles starts before their eighth birthday. She should know what sanitary products are and how to properly use them. Teenage girls should know they have seven secretion points and where their clitoris, urethra, vagina, and anus are located.

Teens should know if anything bad or sexually inappropriate happens, they can tell their mother and/or father immediately without fear of judgment or blame. A lot of the times girls don't tell because the person who violates them is often a family member, their mother's man, or a close friend of the family.

Far too often a young girl getting her period is viewed as something bad and she feels embarrass as opposed to being celebrated. Parents fear their little girl is going to get pregnant. Yes, she can, but it's important to talk with her about the hormones and the urges to have sex that she will experience. Let her know there are safe ways for her to explore her body by herself.

It's okay for boys to do so, and we as women must embrace that girls should engage in self-pleasuring while they're still virgins.

Let's eradicate the stigmatism and educate girls on masturbation. She shouldn't have sex before experiencing her first orgasm. Girls are chastised while boys are praised after having their first sexual experience. In fact, boys are encouraged to get their first piece of pussy. Boys are taught to disrespect females before their initial encounter. On the other side of a teenage boy fucking until he ejaculates (if he's even a teenager yet) is someone's daughter who could possibly become pregnant.

Society, mainly men, have stripped females of their sexual power, rendering females dependent upon men for pleasure. Boys and men are undereducated and disrespectful, yet often the initiator when it comes to sex.

Can you picture a female not feeling the need to have some inexperienced, clueless boy with a hard-on ram his dick inside of her virgin pussy? Boys are not thinking about babies. Sex the first time isn't fun for a girl. Most boys don't care as much about her as he cares about being her first.

Dicks are dumb. Boys just want to cum! Men too. In order to exhibit baby doll love, she lets them.

A Teenage Girl Gets Pregnant

Hang in there with me. Everything I'm building on sets the foundation for that good woman men claim they're looking for. Men who write dating books tremendously fail women. Why? Men want us to be the woman they want us to be, not the woman they make us become from their mental, physical, and financial abuse. Boys/men who abandon pregnant girls/women think parenthood is a fucking game. It's not!

Girls/women have a right to be angry, bitter, and/or disenchanted. And men don't have the decency to apologize to the women they've fucked over because they're too busy ruining/fucking another, and another, and yes, another girl/woman.

Immediately, when a girl becomes pregnant, everyone believes it's her fault. I say, "No it's not." Where's the boy (or man) that's the father of her child? Out looking for a good woman?

The girl's parents may yell, "Didn't I tell you not to do it?" I ask, "Tell her what?" Don't do it? There's a difference between telling a young girl and teaching her how to value her vagina.

Dare I be presumptuous here and say she's done what she was taught; but, perhaps, one of the most crucial lessons of all, to know and value her vagina, was never given to the person who should've passed it along. If I had had a daughter, I can say with certainty, I would've reared her with the spirit in which I'm penning these pages, wishing that someone would've imparted wisdom without judgment to me.

HoneyBHonest: Would you give your toddler son a baby doll? Why or why not?

Parents, family, and friends who gift dolls, doll houses with kitchens, pots, and pans to a little girl for her birthday or Christmas should give more thought to their reason. Even if you told her about sex, the potential psychological impact could have her believing it's okay for her to be objectified by men.

Sweet 16 Isn't Always So Sweet

Many young girls, myself included, have been molested, raped, and/or assaulted by a boy/man before we turn sixteen. Countless women have told me that they were raped but never told anyone. One out of three females are abused in their lifetime. For many reasons, including the male threatening to kill the girl's family member(s), these girls may never tell anyone and the scumbags move on to their next victim.

If something with your child doesn't seem right, do not ignore your gut instinct. No matter how uncomfortable the conversation may be, have it immediately. Don't wait. If your daughter tells you she's been sexually assaulted, regardless to who did it, listen, believe, and support her. Do not judge or degrade her.

My great-grandfather would request/invite my sister and I to visit him in what we called the country (Amite, Louisiana) during the summer. He was over ninety-years-old when he molested my sisters and me. I was seven. Neither of us was comfortable to tell our perspective guardians. Later, Pops came to live with his daughter, my great-aunt and his molestation of me started again.

The worst part was I was more afraid to tell an adult, than I was for it to happen again. I didn't think anyone would believe me. One day my great-aunt walked into the living room and I was on the sofa on my knees doggie-style. My head was pressed against the wall, my pink panties were pulled to the side as Pop rubbed his uncircumcised dick up and down my vaginal area.

My great-aunt beat Pop really bad with a baseball bat. I didn't see, but heard him hollering. I was happy she'd done what I couldn't and that was, whup his ass! I thanked God the molestation ended. I still think if I'd told her, she wouldn't have believed me. I'm not the only woman with such a story at such an early age. Many girls and women suffer in silence because society does not encourage females to speak out about sexual abuse.

Parents and guardians much teach girls (and boys) what sexual abuse is. Any inappropriate sexual touch, online predatory acts, drugging, luring are dangerous and the child must feel comfortable telling the parent. Many situations can be deescalated if the parent is made aware. Dicks are manipulative and girls are confused about what's the right way to tell the appropriate person.

HoneyBHonest: Taking away dolls won't keep our girls from being easily influenced by boys and men, but teaching girls how to love themselves is a good place to start.

At sixteen I was raped at knife-point on the streets of my hometown in New Orleans. He forced me into a dark lot filled with broken down cars. He penetrated me while I was on my period, then he forced me to suck his dick. I thought he was going to kill me afterward. I remember asking God, "Please don't let me die like this." Some women aren't fortunate enough to survive after being raped by their attacker. Others, like my mother, for many reasons, commit suicide. My mom's cause of death was a toxic overdose.

When I was raped, I spoke out. Since my great-aunt had protected me from her own father, I trusted she'd believe what had happened was true. My great-aunt called the police. I gave the police a report in front of her. When I told the officer that my rapist made me perform oral sex, he asked, "What's oral sex?" The officer knew. He just wanted to make sure that at sixteen, I understood what I was saying.

I explained in detail how my rapist made me suck his dick, but I was surprised my great-aunt didn't know what oral sex was. I was no stranger to performing the act because I'd done so a few times with my high school boyfriend. While I'm extremely knowledgeable about sex, I didn't learn a damn thing about sex at home.

Hopefully, I've inspired ladies to talk in depth about sex with their daughters, nieces, cousins, etc. Until women become outspoken, men—even the trusted ones who rape and molest—will get a free pass to abuse the next female.

We don't tell because we hear that we must have done something to cause a boy/man to stick his dick inside of us. Our clothes are too revealing. We hang around boys too much. Women don't want to believe their husband/man is a liar, cheater, abuser so they stand by their man, not their child. Other women don't want to imagine the guy they're dating is a rapist so they never ask, "Have you ever raped or forced a girl/woman to have sex with you?"

If the statistics that one out of three women have been sexually assaulted are true, then every woman cannot be married to, having sex with, or dating an upstanding guy. There's absolutely no justification for any man violating a female's body, but lots of women are in-love with strangers. Even women put girls down by saying she's too fast. She had it coming. She deserved it. Some of these same women are the ones that were beaten, cheated on, and/or degraded. Yet, some women have baby doll love and will do anything for their man as if they've given birth to him.

HoneyBHonest: When you don't know better, you can't do better.

Leave the dolls on the shelves. If women stop buying babies for their babies, maybe their babies won't have a baby by a boy who doesn't give a fuck about her.

Recommended Reading:
He's Just a Friend by Mary B. Morrison

4
Interview with a Dick

This is a mock interview with a dick to give ladies insight as I've had countless conversations with men of various nationalities. I have found there are some differences based on culture. This conversation is for fun.

A man and woman meet on an online dating site. It's their first lunch date at a nice restaurant. They are seated outdoors. It's a hot summer day. They recently finished eating and are enjoying cocktails and conversation. She has on a white maxi halter sundress. He's wearing all black— a fitted short-sleeved shirt, jeans, and leather square-toed shoes.

> *Man: You look better in person. That dress is sexy as hell (stares at her cleavage).*
> *Woman: Thanks for lunch. I like your style (smiles at him).*
> *Man: Wanna come to my house? Watch a movie or something?*
> *Woman: Or something? Can you be more specific?*
> *Man: You know. Whatever you want to do is cool. I can give you a nice massage.*

Woman: What you really want is to fuck my good pussy.

Man: (Smiles.) Any man would be a fool to turn you down.

Woman: You got condoms?

Man: I'm HIV free. Got my papers, but I can stop and get condoms if you want.

Woman: (Smirks.) You wanna fuck raw?

Man: (Nods.) That'd be appreciated. My man here is allergic to latex.

Woman: Hm. Okay.

Man: (Pulls out his credit card and requests the check.) I hate dating sites.

Woman: Ever been married?

Man: Once.

Woman: Divorced?

Man: (Exhales then nods.) She got the house, car, all that. I'm good, though.

Woman: You want to marry me?

Man: (silently stares off to the side thinking) Bitch, I don't know you. If I tell the truth and curse her out I'm going home alone. Again. Best not to answer. (Sighs then picks up his cell, scans the dating app.)

Woman: Nice watch.

Man: (Nods, then smiles while tagging a few females as favorites.)

Woman: The cost of rearing a child from birth through college, your half is roughly $276,000. If you get me pregnant, can you handle that?

Dicks are Dumb

Man: Hell, no (puts down his cell). How the fuck she come up with that number? You crazy. This is our first date.
Woman: (Softly.) You want some pussy?
Man: (Stares at her breasts.) You a tease. What you wanna do?
Woman: Sorry, I don't fuck for free.
Man: Free? I just spent $75.00 on your ass.
Woman: (Sighs heavily.) Exactly.

For $75.00 (or less), he wants to fuck raw. Most men don't inquire if a woman is using any form of birth control. They view her as the sole responsible party for protecting herself from conceiving his child. One hot summer night can leave a woman over a quarter of a million dollars in debt.

Babies aren't free! Men don't think about the cost of providing for their child. A lot of guys either refuse or avoid paying child support. Ladies, stop fucking, then hoping, that he'll like you.

HoneyBHonest: A man with his hand out needs to put his dick in it.

Ladies, you don't have to have the conversation in this chapter, but I suggest before you spread, ask enough questions to find out where his heads are. I don't care if he's single, married, unemployed, or a billionaire, too many men feel entitled to fuck your good pussy for free, but they do not feel obligated (or have the decency) to do right by you should you become pregnant with his child.

Dicks are dumb. What I mean by 'right' is his accepting responsibility for his actions. Respecting you after he has sex with you. Calling (or texting) the same or next day is considerate. If he doesn't call, he doesn't care.

Picking up the entire tab for a minimum of three dates should be the norm for any guy. I've dated men who pick up the tab 100% of the time. Sides chicks should never touch their purse. I'll explain why later.

HoneyBHonest: If he has a main, he's not your man.

Ladies, it's wise to learn how to interview a dick. When you look into a man's eyes, have a conversation with his manhood. Don't take his responses personally. Understand where his compliments, advances, and complaints are coming from. Keep in mind most men have low self-esteem. If you verbally attack him, his dick will hide behind his balls. Your goal is to determine if he's worthy of one: your time; and two: penetrating your good pussy. The best way to protect your vagina is to get to know the man first. It doesn't take long to assess his intentions. If all he wants is sex, he will move fuck you and move on quickly to the next woman. Perhaps, in the same day or night. Stop spreading for guys who are unworthy.

Keep in mind that lots of men claim they're looking for a good woman. Most of them are lying. What a man is hoping to do is make you prove yourself worthy of being his woman when all he really wants to do is get laid. That's why it's imperative if you want a relationship to take your time and get to know his dumb as dick. Take your time. I'll never give you a limit because every situation is unique.

I met a guy on a dating site. Went out with him three times. Enjoyed each date. I asked him when was the last time he'd had sex. He told me he hadn't had sex in over a year. Post his twenty-three-year marriage he'd had two long-term relationships and he believed in being faithful.

I told him, you're lying and I'll tell you why. Every time we went out, at the end of every date he persistently tried to have sex with me. Watch what a man does, ladies. I rejected his advances each time, including the day I let him stay the night. We were naked in bed and nothing happened. I only have sex if I want to and I'd told him before he opted to stay that nothing was going to happen. Ladies, if a man is constantly trying to have sex with you, you are not the only one he's trying to fuck. If he's not properly prepared to have safe sex with you, again, you're not the only one he's fucking raw. He didn't respond because both of us knew he was lying about the last time he'd had sex. Men don't expect women to check them on their shit. I do. You should too.

If you listen carefully and let a man talk more than you, you'll find that most men cannot (or will not) articulate what they want from you. Outside of intercourse, he can't clearly tell you what he means by *right* or *good* as it relates to the type of woman he alleges to want. If he rattles it off to impress you, it's scripted and feeds each female the same lies.

For example. I passed this guy in the mall. I was on the phone talking with my son who lives in Dubai. I could tell, and told my son, by the way that guy looked at me, he was going to approach me. Twenty minutes later, he found me in the back of a store where I was shopping. We exchanged numbers. Later that night, he called. Immediately, after I answered, he said, "If you found the man of your dreams, a man that would give you everything you wanted, treated you like a queen, made love to you, worshiped you, cooked and cleaned for you, would you commit to him?"

I had to tell this motherfucker, "First, you didn't say you would do any of those things, but let's assume you're that guy. Why the fuck are you available?" I asked him to text me a picture.

I googled him. The photo he sent me came up with a heading that included his name stating he was wanted for conning an elderly man out of $40,000. I sent him the article and that fool told me, it was a family misunderstanding. "Fuck you! I'm done!" Guys are liars! Their dicks are their spokesperson when it cums to dealing with women.

HoneyBHonest: I don't think men disappoint women as much as women are too trusting.

You're not trying to change him. Your goal is to understand him and decide if he's right for you. Here's a different interview.

Woman: Are you looking for a woman like your mother?

Man: For sho, but they don't make 'em like her no more. Women these days are lazy.

Regardless of his answer, follow up with, "Why do you feel that way?" Or, "Why not?" Sometimes you'll learn he didn't have a good relationship with his mother.

Woman: So, if you found a woman like your mom, you wouldn't want her to suck your dick. Would you? Just asking.

Man: (Laughs while shaking his head.)

You're not trying to offend him. A lot of men don't give serious thought to their canned answers, so make him rethink or elaborate. Men need to stop trying to find a woman like their mother. Babies need their mommies, not men. Hopefully, he has a sense of humor and won't become angry.

Woman: Okay, let's say you're not exactly looking for a woman like your mother. What type of woman do you really want?

Most men claim they want a hard-working, dedicated, housecleaning, floor sweeping, respectable woman, that can cook her ass off, to marry and have babies with. For most of that they can hire a maid.

Dicks are Dumb

Men want two types of women. Some want a shiny female on their arm and not necessarily a gold-digger, but a gold-digger will suffice if she's supermodel status. Others want a woman that can financially support herself (and sometimes him) so he doesn't have to break his bank account or his back at a nine-to-five (if he has either). This type of guy takes, "Why buy the cow, if you can get the milk for free," to the higher level because he will marry the homely woman and screw other women. Just because a woman holds down her man does not mean he'll be faithful.

Woman: Are you happy with yourself and your life?

You must ask that question. Men love to pursue ladies that are fun, successful, thriving, avid travelers and so forth. When they meet a joyful woman, slowly they steal her zest for life by imposing their expectations and dumping their psychological baggage on her.

The things he loves about you in the beginning are often the same things he despises later, especially if you're a confident woman. He doesn't want you dressing too sexy or being too friendly with others. He feels less of a man if you make more money but he may not admit it. Instead, he constantly talks about what he's going to do to make money and he gets upset if he thinks you're not being supportive of his bright ideas. Slowly his failures become your fault.

HoneyBHonest: When you tone it down to the point where you're miserable, he's happy.

Ladies, stay upbeat throughout the conversation when getting to know a man. If you find that he's depressing or stressing you out, don't dwell on his unhappiness. It's not your responsibility to save him from himself.

Remember you're interviewing his dick. That's the motherfucker you have to know. When a man is depressed, so is his dick. If he cums inside of you, his semen transfers his negative energy into your womb.

HoneyBHonest: If a man isn't happy with himself, his dick will never be content with you.

While it's important to keep an open mind, you must start with the end in mind. That means, you need to know what you want from this dick before he puts the head in. Do you want to be his woman, his wife, or his convenience? Do you want to be the one he's cheating on or the one he's cheating with? Please don't let him decide.

Based on his responses to your questions, determine your level of interest. On your first date, don't give him too many details about what you do, where you live, how many kids you have or want, and definitely don't talk about your exes. You want to know about his exes but not on the first date. If he mentions an ex, tell him, "I'm interested in getting to know you, not her. You can tell me about her some other time." Leave the door open for that discussion. Men who constantly blame their ex for the breakup generally still have feelings for her.

Too many women think ex bashing means there's a good chance to snag the man. Don't be desperate. Interview his dick. Be a good listener. He's telling you who he is.

When women tell guys about their exes, men automatically start comparing themselves to that guy. If they conclude they don't measure up, they will emotionally checkout. Oh, he'll still have sex with you but all you're going to get...is screwed.

You might start off thinking you really like how smart he is but eventually you may deduce his end game is lame. He's trying to convince you to give him brain or let him put the head in.

First encounters and first dates are important. Dicks have one eye. Make sure you're dressed deliciously. Dazzling eyelashes and succulent lipstick will make him focus on your eyes and mouth when you're speaking. Don't be offended if he doesn't hear a damn word. Being a dickstraction can work to your advantage as you make mental notes of what he says.

Go someplace fun. I prefer going to upscale bars, restaurants with tablecloths that are not too busy, or brunch where they serve bottomless mimosas. A nice scenic drive or casual stroll can keep the mood flowing in a positive direction but I don't do free shit on first dates. If a man won't feed you but has time to fuck you, he's not interested in you. He's interested in your vagina.

Ladies, you control the tempo of the conversation. Don't ask him all of these questions at once. Randomly ask some of the questions face-to-face and others over the phone. Also, create your personal list of things *you* want to know about a man.

> *Woman: What do you like most about women?*
> *Man: Her personality.*
> *Dick: Pussy.*
> *Woman: What do you love most about her personality?*
> *Man: You know. I just don't like drama.*
> *Dick: New pussy. More than one pussy at a time. Shit like that.*
> *Woman: You have any kids?*
> *Man: Got a few women trying to say I'm the daddy.*
> *Dick: I got three.*
> *Woman: Where are the kids?*
> *Man: With their mamas.*

Dick: Damn, kiss her! I just want to fuck.

Woman: Do you support them?

Man: Would you pay a car note for a car that's not yours?

Dick: One too light. The other one got autism or something. Nobody in my family look like or got that. Touch her titty.

Woman: Don't touch my breasts.

Man: What?

Dick: Why not?

Woman: I don't like your touch.

Man: Then damn baby. Teach me.

Dick: Touch her pussy.

Woman: (Blocks his hand.) You believe in monogamy?

Man: (Looks around as though the question was intended for someone else.)

Dick: No. There's too many fine women, I can't focus.

Woman: Is that a no?

Man: No what?

Dick: No what?

Woman: Let's move on. Tell me about the most beautiful woman you've dated. What attracted you to her?

Man: (A smile crosses his face.) Aw man. I fucked that up. She was a model. Tall, long legs, nice breasts shaped like honeydew melons. She has ass for days and those dick-sucking lips. (Silence.)

Dick: (Protrudes.)

Woman: Why did the relationship end?
Man: I told you. I fucked up.
Dick: Fucked her girlfriend. But her girlfriend was fine as hell too.
Woman: What do you need in order to be fulfilled in a relationship?
Man: I need a good woman.
Dick: Touch her titty again and tell her whatever it takes to get me in!
Woman: Don't do that. Can you explain?
Man: Women these days act like men. I need one that knows her place. How to treat me like a king. Have my back. Sex me real good. Can't stand no loose or lazy pussy. Truth be told she doesn't have to be supermodel fine as long as she's down for me.
Dick: Wake me when she's done. If she's not putting out, put that bitch out and jack me off. Wish I could slide down your throat so you'll stop with all the questions.
Woman: Why did your last relationship end?
Man: Started treating me like a kid. Telling me what I could and couldn't do. Checking my phone. My computer. Questioning my social posts and DMing my female friends. She was so busy trying to keep a trace she couldn't keep pace. Had to let her go.
Dick: Text and see if we can hit that pussy tonight.
Woman How was your first sexual experience and how old were you at the time?

Man: (exhales long and slow) I was ten. She was around thirteen. Said she wanted to see my thing. Didn't know she was going to lick it. When I felt her lips, I was scared. Real talk. When my body released white fluids I thought I was going to die. She stole my innocence. Women think guys want that, but honestly, I never saw females the same after that.

Dick: Bitch please!

Woman: Is that the reason men have a hard time being faithful?

Man: (hunches his shoulders) Most of the time I don't know what I want. It's easy to stay with one woman. Hard to be with just one. I think I can be faithful, then an attractive female smiles at me all friendly and shit, then when I hit that, once, twice. After a few times with her, I'm bored.

Dick: Contrary to popular belief, I get bored too.

Woman: Do you think you'll ever be monogamous?

Man: Why should I?

Dick: Next question.

Woman: Then you cool with your woman sexing another man?

Man: Hell no! It's her fault I cheat. I can't stand that on again off again shit. One minute she's all-in. The next day she hates my fucking ass. Don't want me touching my pussy. She tells me to leave, then beg me to stay.

Dicks are Dumb

Dick: Can we just fuck?
Woman: Well, dick. I mean, dude. Thanks for your time.

HoneyBHonest: Always know what you want ladies. If you don't know what you want, you will end up with a dick instead of a man who has a dick.

Recommended Reading:
Darius Jones by Mary B. Morrison

II

The Three Rings

5
Relationship Ring

What the hell is a relationship ring? Let me say this first, a woman should never buy her own relationship, engagement, or wedding ring. Never. Men like everything easy, especially their women.

As soon as a man asks a woman to be his lady, he should already have a budget in place to purchase his girl a relationship ring, immediately. Yes, a man is supposed to get a woman a ring when he wants to take her good pussy off the dating market. And no, the guy does not get to pick it out. She does!

The ring should be on a woman's finger no more than one week after a guy asks her to be his lady. If he's serious, there shouldn't be any hesitation. The problem nowadays is men have got shit twisted. They hollering like bitches. "Do I get a ring too?" Let me answer for her. Hell no!

Men are quick to ask, "What's in it for me? What does she bring to the table?" If he doesn't know, masturbation is always available to him and his dumb ass dick. Whatever his reason, a man knows why he wants to date a woman. Stop minimizing her value. Buy the ring!

Society makes it easy for men to use women for everything from pussy to paying all his bills. Men want to lay their heads on a woman whenever they want. If a man doesn't feel you're worthy of a relationship ring ladies, he thinks less of you as a woman.

Guys always feel as if a woman holds him to a standard, or expects him to provide for his child, she's trying to use him. He bitches that she's using his child support money to get her hair and nails done. WTF! She had that on point when she met you dude. What men really trip off of is his ex being fucked by another man.

Men fuck over women, leave the woman, then they want her to be miserable for not staying with him. Buy the ring dude. It can only elevate your status. Dudes worry about getting played when all the fuck they do is play games. What they're really scared of is karma biting them in their ass. Men don't feel used when they're sitting at a woman's table eating her food.

Men want to know if the relationship doesn't work out does he get the ring back? Hell no! Once he puts the ring on his woman's finger, it's hers. Again, dude, you don't have to spend a fortune but get something nice that she won't be embarrassed to wear. Do not pick out any fake shit, ladies!

Women, you have got to stop voluntarily taking yourself out of the dating game for a loser. The less desperate a woman is, the more interested the guy becomes in her. Stop claiming men that aren't committed to you. Do not commit to him if he's not willing to invest in you.

Some of my gurls are with the right man. But that doesn't mean your daughter, sister, or girlfriends will be as fortunate. Please, if you feel someone needs to read my book, buy them a copy.

A relationship ring is not an engagement ring ladies. When you get it, don't go running around lying about you're engaged.

That's ring number two, where the man spends two months of his annual salary, gets down on one knee, and asks for your hand in marriage. A woman should receive three rings from her man, but the truth is the majority of women who are dating will never get one, even if she stays with her man for years.

Guys want women to feel anxious about the alleged shortage of dicks. Fuck all that— there's fifty men to every woman. That's some male misogynist bullshit to make men feel superior. The world—planet earth—is your playground ladies. Stop putting all your options in one man at a time. With the exception of broke, stop saying I only date men who are, black, white, tall, short, rich, poor, etc.

HoneyBHonest: No ring. No relationship.

Most men date for convenience, not for commitment. And honestly, ladies should have fun dating too. Women make it extremely easy for men not to give them anything, especially a ring.

Old single men get lonely. They have male enhancements (that might kill them) in one hand, and their dick in the other. Enhancement drugs aren't as fun as men make it seem. Some of the side effects are: headaches, damage to the urethra, permanent difficulty maintaining an erection, permanent problems with urination, penis fractures, vision changes, runny nose, congestion, dizziness, digestive problems, body and back pain. Most men feel the benefits outweigh the risks.

HoneyBHonest: Pussy has power.

Many old guys are financially unstable but they want a pretty young thing they cannot sexually satisfy. Gurls if you're in that type of relationship, demand the ring and get you a fine young side dude that don't need enhancements to maintain an erection. If your old man has assets, put your name on everything from his bank account to his house, and cars.

Too many women have low expectations. Know your worth. If you're going to have a baby out of wedlock, choose the father wisely. Make sure he's in a position to contribute his half, $276,000.

Most Americans have never heard of a relationship ring. Yet, in other countries, it's tradition. I created the requirement before I learned that in parts of Africa, couples date to marry; therefore, the guy buys his girlfriend/fiancée a ring to show she's unavailable to other men.

One day it dawned on me. Some women stay in a relationship and the man never respects her enough to put a ring of any kind on her finger. I started asking the men I knew if they would buy their woman the ring. The ones with money who owned car dealerships, restaurants, coached professional sports, or had a great paying job, said, "Yes." My male friends balling on a budget said, "No," hella fast.

HoneyBHonest: The mindset of a man often matches the size of his wallet.

An increasing number of women will never marry, especially the Millennials. Not because young ladies don't want to have a husband. Guys don't get serious because they feel they haven't found the right person, they aren't financially stable, or they're not ready to settle down. Hopefully, young men won't wait until their dicks stop working to put a ring on a woman's finger.

HoneyBHonest: Friends with benefits vanished, because men were the real beneficiaries.

The relationship ring goes on the right ring finger, not the left. If you've read my novel, *Soulmates Dissipates*, self-published June 2000, and republished by Kensington Publishing Corporation, June of 2001, you're familiar with Wellington Jones giving Jada Diamond Tanner, a relationship ring. He placed the ring on her right finger then later, he took the ring off of her right ring finger, proposed in front of his mother, then placed the same ring on her left ring finger.

A different ring for the engagement is nice but not necessary, as many men do not have discretionary income to purchase two, let alone three nice rings—although a woman is worthy of all three.

One out of every two men I asked confessed that although they hadn't heard of a relationship ring, they would not only buy the ring but thought it was a nice idea. Twenty-five percent said they'd buy a necklace or tennis bracelet but definitely not a ring. And the other twenty-five percent immediately said no, and started complaining.

The psychiatrist I dated was so excited about my concept he consulted with a female friend on what ring to buy me because he wanted to get something really nice. Over dinner, he presented me with a beautiful ring and matching earrings. We dated for a while. I stopped seeing him because although he bought the ring, he was still in-love with his wife, and wanted his family back. They were separated, living apart, and going through a divorce. He was lonely. I was his soundboard, but never his bed partner. I'd like to think I helped him to appreciate his wife and son before his divorce was final. Sometimes women make men better for another woman. Indeed, I kept the ring and earrings, but he never once asked for them back. One day, he just stopped calling.

For the guys who said no to buying me a relationship ring, that was okay. I continued going out with them but let them know I was not exclusive. One guy bought me a wine basket instead of a ring. I love a good cabernet but he must've purchased the cheapest wine he could find. I couldn't give it away. Trust me, I tried. One bottle of something I preferred would've been better than four big bottles that I hated. Men need to observe what their woman likes.

I've been married, and proposed to (once officially), several unofficial (which in my opinion never counts). You know that, "Will you marry me?", but the question didn't accompany a ring bullshit. Either a man proposes with a ring or shouldn't propose at all.

HoneyBHonest: Ask for the relationship ring, ladies. It's no if you don't ask.

The man who is serious about taking you off the dating market will put a relationship ring on your finger when he asks you to become exclusive because he understands the symbolism. He gets it. He wants to respect you. Please don't take him for granted. This is not about building your ring collection. Real men don't mind doing the right thing but no man wants to be used.

In fact, some guys would do this for their lady today without hesitation, if he knew what a relationship ring meant. Ladies you have to inform your guy. When he asks you to be his woman, his lady, or to be exclusive, ask if he's heard of a relationship ring and let him know you'd really like to have one.

HoneyBHonest: Ask for what you want.

Recommended Reading:
Soulmates Dissipate by Mary B. Morrison

6
Engagement Ring

Ladies, start your relationship with the outcome in mind. Dangle the pussy. Tease him. Mind fuck him! Learn what he likes in and out of bed. Become his best friend and his best lover, in that order. Never show him all your sex skills upfront. Every now and then, introduce something new to him. Be inconsistent on purpose. When a man doesn't know what to expect, anticipation keeps him interested in you.

Most men enjoy foot massages but a lot of guys have never had a woman do that. While watching television, or sharing quality time, get some oil, and stroke his feet. Don't do it again for at least three months. Next time, do his hands. Pace and space things out. Make sure he's doing for you first. Your pampering, cooking, whatever you do to keep him happy, is a reward. Like training a dog, treats are given after good behavior is exhibited, not before.

If a woman jumps in trying to fuck the shit out of a guy, sucking his dick really good, cooking for him, and cleaning his place, she is not wife material. When he wants to fuck, or needs his house cleaned, he'll call the easy chick that will do anything to please him. When he wants to take someone out on a date, he'll call the woman that massaged his feet instead of fucking him because she intrigues him.

Let's face it. A man is going to do one of two things. Some guys are going to buy his woman an engagement ring and propose. Other men are never going to make that purchase or ask for his woman's hand in marriage for a number of reasons.

The number one reason is, his woman has proven that no matter what he does, she's not going anywhere. Next, he's convinced her he's the best she can do. Then, there are the guys who are losers. He's a control beasts that doesn't mind using women and will take all he can, then proudly leave his woman broke and broken. The more she begs him to come back, the more he takes from her.

Some women are never going to get the ring. Lots of women do all the right things, but they do them for the wrong man. Women have to know when to bail. Dudes tell everyone except their woman, "I'm not going to marry her." In my opinion, those types of guys are bitches.

HoneyBHonest: Women are often unaware of how their man truly feels.

Ladies, just because a man is with you does not mean he loves or is in-love with you. Realistically, a woman could be a seat-filler until his Mrs. comes along. If he believes there is someone better for him, he's not going to give the woman he's with an engagement ring. He doesn't believe his woman is worthy of being his wife, and he's not taking himself off the market.

I'm going to keep asking my gurls, "What do you want?"

Stop allowing a man to define what you deserve. Ask yourself if the ring is more important than having the man. Most women want both. Every woman doesn't want or need a ring and every woman does not want to be married (or married again).

HoneyBHonest: Women get what they negotiate.

A relationship is no different. Hone in on your negotiating skills. If you want to marry your guy, the sooner you discuss his intentions the better. Notice, I didn't say the sooner you discuss marriage. Talking about marriage won't matter if he never intends to get married.

A man gets down on one knee for the woman who takes care of his heads and his heart.

A woman has to know her man. If the female screams, cries, rips up her guy's shit, busts the windows out of his car, and the guy stays with her, he loves, and may ask her to marry him. He understands he's to blame for lying, cheating, and provoking her. I don't recommend that a woman accept a ring from this kind of man because he's never going to stop breaking her heart.

Dicks are dumb. Unfortunately, some men are too.

When a man holds a woman's hand, and opens the ring box, most women are usually thrilled that he asked. Out of excitement she's nodding before he gets out the question. She tells him that it's beautiful, she loves him and marriage is what she wants. But if a lady lets a man slide an engagement ring on her finger just to get the ring, or spare her man from humiliation, the marriage will be based on a lie.

Too many females are in unhealthy relationships, but all that goes out the window when they're blinded by the bling. If he's cheating or beating on his woman, giving her a ring won't make him stop. If she's arguing all the time, checking his cell, trying to track his every move, if she has trust issues, she's not ready for a legal commitment. Couples should resolve serious problems before standing at the altar.

Engagement is an opportunity to grow closer to your mate. Let the ring remind you of why you fell in-love. No relationship is perfect, but if you're unhappy before you accept his engagement ring don't expect having the ring to make things better. Work on your engagement so the marriage won't be a chore.

Women who believe the ring will turn a frog into a Prince when they kiss their groom are destined for divorce court. Engagement is serious business. Stay focused on uplifting one another.

I was in a seven-year relationship with my soulmate from the ages of 25-32. We truly had a September Virgo love/hate union. Our birthdays are one day apart.

I've always had the mindset that I will never treat a man better than he treats me. Being with my ex was at times, pure insanity. Our lives were drama driven to the tenth power. The good times with our friends were plentiful, but any moment things could go from hot to hell. He was six feet, six inches tall, managed a club, and was a standout at every, and I do mean every gathering. I enjoyed being his woman. But my ex, like most men, cheated but couldn't handle me going out with other men. The difference was, he tried to hide his indiscretions. Once I found out about his other women, I started dating other men.

I still believe in letting a man set the tone for a relationship. I let guys know upfront, if you're fucking, I'm fucking. Whatever a man does to me, will be done unto him.

HoneyBHonest: Women do not have to be the better person when men fuck up.

My ex planned a cozy picnic on the waterfront, pulled out a beautiful diamond ring, and asked me to marry him. Before he could put the engagement ring on my finger, my response was very candid. I told him, no. His proposal was too late, yet sobering. The bad times could've landed either one us behind bars. I didn't want to live the rest of my life with him. A year later, he married. They got pregnant. Somewhere during his marriage to her he circled back to me. Told me he didn't want any more kids. His boys were eighteen. She didn't have any children. He didn't care. He convinced her to have an abortion. She did and regretted it. Later they divorced.

When the ring is more important than the man, women need to say no to both. Women have to dig into a bag of dicks to get the right man to propose.

A man knows if a woman is the one, but a woman needs to find out why he feels that way. Is he the right one? Listen to what he's not saying. Pay attention to what he does. Don't be foolishly in love. Trust your instincts.

An engagement ring may need to be returned depending on why the engagement ends. I know some women feel entitled to keep the engagement ring, however that's not automatically the case, such as it is with the relationship ring. One of my ex-boyfriends asked me to wear his ring and think about marrying him. I agreed to give the engagement consideration. My final decision remained the same and I gave the ring back.

Sometimes keeping the ring after a man requests the ring back is meaningless.

Respect your engagement as you would your marriage. Be happy more than you're sad. Don't stay upset. Try not to become angry. Never hate your mate.

Now if a woman proposes to her man—which I don't recommend—buy him a ring, but quietly do it with his money. If he calls off the engagement, let him keep the ring.

Recommended Reading:
Never Again Once More by Mary B. Morrison

7
Wedding Ring

Do you really want to be his wife?
Marriage is easy to get into; hard as fuck to get out of.

If a woman seriously wants the wedding ring, she has to stay ahead of her dick. Most couples don't divorce over infidelity. It's the backlash of infidelity that rips a hole in people's heart. A lot of marriages end in divorce because a man's dick suffers from ADDD (Attention Deficit Dick Disorder).

Cheating creates the demise and causes dissension. Next thing you know, you're questioning his whereabouts, wondering if he's with her, why did he do it, and will he cheat on you again? Yes, your husband will continue to get dickstracted. Men think about sex all the time. I believe one of the guys who wrote a relationship book for women divorced his wife and married his mistress.

HoneyBHonest: Most men don't remember their vows.

Wedding vows are meaningless, if they're not taken seriously. Ladies, when you first learn that your man has had an affair, calmly discuss right away if he wants an open relationship. Of course, he's more than likely going to say, no. That usually means he'll continue sexing other women and try to hide it from you. But no way does he want you to have a side dude. The conversation regarding infidelity must be addressed before standing at the altar. Don't pretend it didn't happen or think he's going to change.

HoneyBHonest: Rings don't make marriages work. People do.

Before you sign the certificate ladies, keep your man focused on you throughout the engagement. Do not track his whereabouts. Nor should you be at his beck and call. When a man messes up, a woman will fail at every attempt to force her man do the right thing. It's a waste of time, but it's what the asshole dudes want. Some men believe if she doesn't cry, she doesn't care. What does a man do to show he cares? He lies.

Save your tears, ladies. A man who is concerned about your feelings will respect you at all times. If you've got the relationship ring, establish a bond with his parents, siblings, kids, his children's mother, his boys, and his female friends. Lock all of them into your phone, by first and last names, addresses, cell numbers, and social pages. A social engagement allows you to easily gather contacts. Take your time. Remember ladies, spying is a waste of your time. Women are smarter than men. You want the information just in case you need it.

Get and keep your man involved in couple and family activities at the beginning of your relationship. When men start to disassociate with home and start investing more time with his boys or going out solo, the marriage shifts to second position. It's not that guys shouldn't do things with their friends, but casual outings should never take priority over what's important to his wife and kids. Ladies, if you keep yourself first, you'll never compete for second place.

HoneyBHonest: Give a man an incentive, not an ultimatum, to marry you.

I cannot emphasize this enough. A woman who pays for the wedding ring because her man can't afford it is doing two things: 1) emasculating her man, and 2) handicapping / enabling her man. Before he says "I do", she's already shown him he does not have to support the household.

You've got the ring. Now what? The man, not the ring, is the prize. Every time you show someone the ring, compliment your man.

Women who feel their marital status solidifies their worthiness stop referring to their man by name, and start saying, "My husband this. My husband that." I don't recommend doing this all the time because 50% of marriages end in divorce. If that should be you, losing your title makes separation tremendously difficult because you lose yourself in the process.

Let's go back to the question, "What do you want"? Do you honestly know? What's most important to you in a marriage? Lots of people say the family unit is primary, but the moment a man or woman has an affair, family unity is the first to be destroyed.

HoneyBHonest: Don't value the pussy or the penis more than the person.

Ladies, if you can sincerely make your mental health a priority, your marriage will be better. Learning to forgive preserves your sanity. Hate and depression destroys women. Stress ages women. Release anything that makes you unhappy. Meditate. Pray. Forgiving someone does not mean what they did was okay, or that you'll stay, but it does allow you to heal and maintain your self-worth. Don't tolerate a man's repeated dysfunctional behavior.

Should a marriage operate like a business? Absolutely. The roles and responsibilities should not only be delineated but also taken seriously. It's not automatically a woman's role to cook, clean, and care for the kids.

Plenty of women make more than their spouse. Just as the finances are shared in the household, other obligations should be as well. I'm not talking about he takes out the trash when he feels like. Or he sits on the couch while you bring him a plate, and after he's finished eating you not only take his plate but you also wash all the dishes, only to do it again day after day.

Ladies, don't start off doing things to impress a man if you don't like doing those things. When your true self evolves, whatever you've masked can lead to your unhappiness later. Don't expect a man to do the same. Men lie to get you, and hope by the time you find out that they don't make as much as money as they told you, they have more kids, or they never played professional sports—that

you love them so much, you won't leave them.

Communicate often and be a great listener. I'm not saying you have to discuss every detail of each day but do ask, "How was your day?" And tell your mate about yours. You don't want to become the couple that stops speaking to one another. Plan vacations. Some people talk about everything except their relationship. Create meaningful dialogue every day in your marriage. Arguing about where you've been, or why didn't you answer your phone is counterproductive.

Know your man well enough to detect based on his energy and body language when something isn't right. You don't have to address every little thing but do not ignore when negative energy enters the room. Try to unveil the underlying cause.

The worst thing you can do is allow outside influences to dictate your feelings for your partner. Some people will be genuinely happy for you. Others will secretly despise you.

Dicks are Dumb

Don't discuss your problems with your friends. Talk with your spouse.

Everyone deserves love and happiness. Women often marry the feeling that the man gives them, not the man.

Realistically, couples can have it all when they fully support one another. Then each person has to do and be their best. Honesty and flexibility are needed.

Having your husband's baby will not make him an active parent. Always be inclusive during your pregnancy. Before the baby is born, use the words *us, we,* and *our* often. This is the perfect stroller for *us. We're* pregnant. *We* have a doctor's appointment. Honey, *our* baby just kicked. Men need to be baby trained. If he has kids that he's not providing for currently, he may do the same with your kids.

Don't anticipate divorce. Prepare for the 'what ifs.'

Overnight, I went from being a wife. to being separated, to divorced, and back to single. I had a good government job. Didn't make a lot of money but we lived in an upscale neighborhood. The owners were generous and our rent was under $300.00 a month. I had him move out. Thankfully, the judge awarded me my car because my ex requested it in the settlement. I let my ex take whatever he wanted out of the apartment, except for the beds. I didn't monitor his move out. I was clear about was what most important to me. My son and I were able to reside in a healthy and happy environment. If I'd stayed in my marriage, I would not be the woman and the writer that I am today.

Answer a few questions before standing at the altar. Does he love you? Do you love him? Are you equally yoked? You can lie to yourself but the truth will come out in a marriage. Men are equal opportunists nowadays and he might dig real deep into your finances if you divorce him.

Is he marrying you for your looks, your money, or what he perceives you can do for him or his career? Why did you accept his proposal? These are all valid questions that a woman should answer before she says, "I do". Every man is not marriage material. Never believe you can change a man.

Marriage should make you better, not bitter.

HoneyBHonest: Get a prenuptial agreement.

Recommended Reading:
Unconditionally Single by Mary B. Morrison

III

What Men Really Want

8
Why Men Cheat

Cheating has little to do with sex. If a man could leave his dick at home, he'd still cheat. Deep down men want to be loved. From their mother, sister, child, woman, men have got to have affection. The kind that makes them feel, not worthy, but wanted.

How many single moms have heard men say, "My child doesn't call me. Why should I call him/her?" That's backward as fuck but men don't care.

Men fear rejection. Lames prefer women pursue them.

Drug lords, preachers, thugs, politicians, soldiers, blue and white collars, billionaires, celebrities, everywhere you look, these men are either married or have a main. I have a friend who works for the FBI. He shared, no specifics, but said a lot of criminals are caught because no matter how long they are on the run, eventually they will go to, not any woman, their woman.

Very few men are truly single. The world of dicks revolves around pussy. A lot of men feel entitled to have more than one woman.

Let's face it. Men are dogs. Not all dogs are bad. Unlike our four legged pets, a man doesn't have to sniff your anus first but he might be kinky enough to do so. Guys are quick to blame their inability to control where they stick their dick on society.

Even the most faithful guy experiences emotional infidelity. I prefer to call it, fantasizing. My NFL head coach friend says, "I like my fantasies in my head, not in my bed." His dirty talking was well above roleplaying. I introduced him to unusual toys and oh boy! I enjoyed him.

HoneyBHonest: Sex should be an experience, not a chore.

I know lots of women would be uncomfortable with a man expressing himself in the sheets if it's not all about her. And, too many women deprive themselves of naughty thoughts.

Have fun ladies! Be outrageously adventurous. Explore your body and your options. I get it why some women try to control their man, but understand that you can't erase the sizzle reel in his brain. Don't try.

A lot of women worry about their man cheating before the relationship begins primarily because they've been cheated on before. When a man looks at another woman or speaks to her, females instantly believe the guy wants to fuck the woman he's looking at. When this happens, I recommend you take notice of an attractive man. If your dude is physically abusive, none of my suggestions are for you.

Confident and trusting women are happier and have fewer relationship problems. How do you become the woman that doesn't worry? You have to learn who you are and change the way you view men.

I have a male family member that's married. His wife came to me and said her husband was taking her for granted. She didn't say he was cheating, but when a man gets off from work at 5:00pm and walks through the door of his house to his family at 2:00am, something is wrong in their marriage.

I told her, "to run away from home and don't tell your husband when you're leaving or where you're at". Leave the kids with him. He's the father. The children will be fine. The reason I told her to leave was simple.

I mentioned this earlier. When you worry more about your man (whether he's cheating or not) he cares less about you.

She packed her bags. Her sister packed her bags. I packed my bags too. We all checked into a suite at a hotel (with a kitchen). I don't cook. They brought gumbo, red beans and rice, salad, breakfast food, and I brought cocktails.

For three days, we listened to and supported the wife. Her husband called about thirty times back-to-back. I told her do not answer the phone. We went to the movies. It was around Christmas time. The wife's cell phone notified her that GPS was installed on her cell. Two minutes later, her sister's cell had tracking added.

We laughed and continued watching the movie. Now the wife was feeling bad. I told her don't worry about him. He'll be okay.

Now I had a little insight to this relationship and once upon a time, the husband had a side. A side that he'd given his wife's laptop to, and offered to buy a car. His wife was not the cheating kind, nor did I or her sister encourage her to do that. The wife needed a temporary (72 hour) emotional and physical separation from her husband to let him experience what his life would be like without her. Plus, she needed to vent.

When we checked out of the hotel and she went home to her husband, I told her he's going to be upset, at first. The more he talks, the more you listen. Do not argue. The louder he speaks, the softer you answer. The first thing he did was accuse her of being with another man.

Dicks are Dumb

Once I spoke with him, gave him an account of all the times he'd called interrupting us, he believed her and realized if he wanted to keep his family, he had to change. Men are foolish and dicks are dumb. After three days, he cared more about if his wife was sharing her pussy than if she was okay.

Your man is more insecure than you. He needs constant reassurance. What is cheating to you? Is it physical? Emotional? Both? And how relevant is infidelity to the success or failure to your relationship?

If infidelity is on your list of deal breakers for your marriage, you may want to exclude for better, or for worse from your vows. It's hard for people who don't know who they are or what they want to make someone else happy.

Men carry the weight of the world on their shoulders. They are concerned about being successful, powerful, desirable, rich, and having material things that attracts pussy. Women carry their man and children on their back.

Sex for men is a way to release their frustrations. His fucking another woman doesn't mean in his head that you're not first. It simply means you're not the only one.

HoneyBHonest: Monogamy is not natural.

If fidelity were the norm, humans would take one mate for life like penguins. Well, if you've read the book, not *King Penguin*.

The first lines of chapter one in my novel, *Somebody's Gotta Be on Top*, are, "Monogamy wasn't natural. Monogamy was a learned behavior that Darius couldn't be taught. When would women realize, sex wasn't a bed partner with love?"

Maybe your man is emotionally deficient. Perhaps sexing one woman bores him. Ejaculating inside of any part of a woman makes him feel powerful. He doesn't like women. He fucks women rough as a form of punishment. He's seldom penalized and often forgiven for his infidelity. He's heard he's like a bull and told, don't run down the hill and fuck one cow. Walk down the hill and fuck *all* the cows. His woman loves him so much she'll accept anything he does, including cheating. He's insecure. He's confused. He can't sustain an erection with you and needs to test-drive his dick with someone else. He's smart, it's his dick that is dumb wants to cum. He doesn't care if his woman leaves him. There's a shortage of men so he's entitled to more than one woman. He works with her, sees her every day, and the building attraction makes him want to bend her the desk and penetrate her. He's a sex addict. He doesn't care how many times he gets caught, he's not going to stop. He claims your withholding sex made him go elsewhere. Regardless, when a man cheats, he convinces himself (in advance) there is always a justification.

What men aren't ready for is Mother Nature's intervention. The average man ejaculates approximately 7,200 times during his lifespan, and approximately 2,000 of those experiences will be from masturbation. Depending on how often a guy is active, the frequent shooters slow down sexually before they turn fifty.

Erectile dysfunction happens and it scares the shit out of guys to think they can't get hard enough to blast off the few seeds in their scrotum. Off to the doctor he goes for a prescription (for male enhancement) that is covered by his health insurance because men have determined that ED is a disease. Yet, some organizations don't cover birth control for women.

While men are often one and done, women can climax for over an hour.

Females don't have ED concerns. Women can use coconut oil (which is natural unlike male enhancement drugs) if they experience vaginal dryness. A man cannot blame bad sex on a woman, but some guys try when they know the real problem is their inability to perform or unwillingness to please.

Ladies, if you don't have game, you will get played. Game is knowledge. Knowledge is power. If men could fuck like women they'd cheat all the damn time. Women are better equipped to experience sexual pleasure. Dumb dicks fuck with one goal and that's to cum.

Men who cheat don't always wear protection. Those guys really are dumb ass dicks!

HoneyBHonest: A woman should never wait for a man to please her.

Recommended Reading:
Somebody's Gotta Be on Top by Mary B. Morrison

9
Sex Galore Doesn't Make Her a Whore

What's an acceptable head count for a lady when it comes to how many bed partners she's had? If you answered that question, you're wrong. The reason being, no one can dictate anyone else's life. Most people want to believe their opinion matters. I say, feel free to express yourself, but after you're all said and done, it will still be your opinion.

Females have more dickatunities than men have pussitunities due to the mere fact that there's always a dick hanging around waiting for a pussy to get in to. Never tell a man your number. If he inquires, ask him how many women has he raped. Only a guy that wants to use a woman's sexual liberation against her, will ask.

A woman who co-signs a man's condemnation of her...is a fool.

Judge not, that ye be not judged. There are no short cuts to acquiring high self-esteem. But there are a million plus ways to let a man dog you out.

Ladies, you shouldn't give a damn about what others think about you, especially men. Dudes who want to control women use sex as their weapon. I'm so fucking over men and their double-standards bullshit!

HoneyBHonest: Thank goodness! Men cannot out sex women.

The male ego has brainwashed countless women into believing men are superior. I want my gurls to make a list of the things men do to dominate and degrade women. Then, next to each statement, explain why you find this to be true. Don't stop there. Have your man and/or guy friends/family write the same about men, not women.

Sight unseen, I bet all of his answers lead back to his dick. When that's the case, tell him to fuck himself. The saddest part is men use their penis to superficially elevate their self-worth. But if all he has going for himself is dick, does that make him a worthless prick?

If all a woman has going for herself is pussy, that bitch should never be broke. Women need to wise up. Have you ever heard of a man being kidnapped, sold into prostitution, or raped for his dick? There's a plethora of documentaries on sexual abuse against women.

I'm disgusted when the first thing that comes out of a trifling man's mouth is, "Women do it to." Do what? These guys don't want to admit all the shit they've done to hurt women, especially the females these men label as whores.

Call her names before you stick your dumb dick in her, then jack your dick! Problem solved.

Once more women start valuing their vagina women around the world can flip the script on sexual domination. Traditional women may never change their ways, but I have tremendous hope for the Millennials. All we need is for the young people to be deprogrammed from social dating norms that are outdated. Society has to stop setting females up for relationship failure by making girls believe they have to cater to a man in order to get a husband—or in many cases, a male dependent.

Females must own their sexuality, travel the globe, and forget about waiting on a man to sweep them off their feet. It's ridiculous for a twenty-year-old to say, "I don't think I'm ever going to get married."

A man who does not fully support his woman is not the huge stuffed animal you thought you won. He's that trinket that is hidden underneath the shelf in a box full of other disappointments. Ladies, open your mind and your eyes and determine a man's worth before you let a man claim you.

The Millennials are more accepting of non-identification of their sexuality. I say, women don't know what they really want or like because so many have permitted men to dicktate who they are. Older women who are set in their ways can learn a lot from the younger females who are starting to adapt to the current dating environment.

HoneyBHonest: Women should masturbate the same as men. Even more.

Here's why I'm disgusted with men!

Men. Men. Men.

Got to have sex. Want to have sex. Lie to get laid. Will stick their dick inside of a woman with or without permission. They rape to cum. They molest their female relatives to cum. They impregnate then abandon women (and their children). They feel entitled to grope a woman's pussy with no consequences. The horrible sexual things men do to little girls, young ladies, and women to ejaculate or mentally masturbate may be frowned upon, but are often ignored or accepted by others.

Men. Men. Men.

Slip drugs into women's drinks to have sex with them. Solicit sex from prostitutes. Go to strip clubs and have sex with strippers. Rape women in the military. Rape females on college campuses. Dumb ass dicks feel justified in their criminal behavior, believing if she dressed a certain way she wanted him.

Men. Men. Men.

Have made pimping and human trafficking of girls and women a billion-dollar business. They couldn't do it without male clients. Men pay and show up at hotel rooms to penetrate a female that has been drugged and repeatedly raped, to have their turn to cum. They sex prostitutes in alleys, cars, anywhere they think they won't get caught.

Men. Men. Men.

Disrespect women. Beat women. Kill women. Over a woman's right to choose not to choose him. If she's not exclusive with him. If she threatens to leave him. He gets angry and wants to make her suffer.

Men are quick to call women whores. The woman that he lays with becomes less than a woman in his eyesight if she has sex with another man. If she enjoys having intercourse with more than one man. All the things men enjoy, they do their best to deny women the same privilege.

HoneyBHonest: If a man could fuck like a woman, all women would be fucked.

Men can lie, cheat, steal, and kill (and most men fit into one of those categories), and justify their actions. With all they do, the one thing men need above all else is the love of a woman. Wife. Side. Mom. Men literally go insane when women reject them.

Who's to blame when a man is ostracized by the woman who once loved him?

Men. Men. Men.

Women are so beautiful yet easily brainwashed. Physical features do not make one woman better than other. Ladies, if you are breathing, you are blessed. Don't envy attractive women for you know not what abuse they have endured. Don't condemn sexually confident women. Do not verbally bash and abuse mistresses and side chicks for it is the man who fucks and fucks over both. Forgive, but stop supporting men who cheat. If you stay with a cheater, own the fact that he is the culprit, and you and the other woman are his victims.

Sex galore does not make her a whore. Stop wasting your life worrying about what or whom your man is doing. Put your sex groove in motion and drive your life toward happiness, Yes, recapture the joy inside of you. Remember, the less you focus on him, the more he'll turn to you.

Ladies, make your fantasy your reality. Start by visualizing intimacy. Whatever that looks like for you. It can simple as the love you want. The life you want. Free of all shame and potential judgement, sexually please yourself. Yes, I'm suggesting women masturbate as often they like.

It's time for women to know their body. Embrace their sexuality. Learn how to turn the spotlight on yourself. You are a star. Shine!

If sex galore is good for him, healthy sex is definitely great for women.

I have a girlfriend that's in a long-term relationship. Her man has become boring in bed according to her. Unmotivated. Doesn't do the things he used to. She suggested to her man that they give each other a pass to have a one-night stand. Immediately, he said no. My guess is he's had quite a few secret sexual encounters, but the visual of another man doing to his woman what he's done to other women, made him outright deny her allowing another man to do what he no longer did. It's his mind, it's his pussy.

Dicks are Dumb

Let's us assume her man has never cheated on her. Is it fair for a man to refuse his woman/wife sexual satisfaction if he is unwilling to try to please her? Keep in mind that men will not be denied sex.

Dicks are dumb.

Men believe women never have casual sex. If a woman allows a man to penetrate her, her guy thinks she's in love with the guy or might fall in-love with him. He fears the other man may be better at pleasing his woman. Basically, men are insecure. They fear competition. Yet, they don't appreciate or value the woman that they have. She's like a trophy on his shelf and he could care less about pleasing her long as when he looks at the mantle, she's still there for him, he's satisfied. His woman could be miserable. He doesn't care enough to change. Long as she doesn't go anywhere, long as she doesn't stop loving him, he's good with that.

For all the guys thinking I'm male bashing, the truth is, I understand you and you don't like me for keeping it real with women. You don't want me putting ideas in your woman's head. You don't want your woman liberating herself sexually.

I pray women no longer accept a man's selfish bullshit and start enjoying safe sex galore. Whether with toys, or a man, before you take off your clothes, make sure your mind is in a healthy space, and you have protection. Date more than you have sex. Use protection each time. Putting a condom on your vibrator will help reduce the chances of getting a bacterial infection.

Men who fuck raw, do so almost all the time. Even when a woman insists they use a condom, a man will find a way to slip, or take it off. I had a guy ask me, "Are you HIV free?" Put on the condom dude because I don't trust that you are.

Men are spreading STDs like wildfire—HIV/AIDS, HPV, HSV, BV, PD, and more—but quickly blaming it on women. Once a woman contracts a disease, she can transfer it a different man (who wants to fuck raw). I still hold men accountable for the majority of STDs because even married men are not shielding themselves during their dumb dick moments.

Ladies, another reason you must know your body is you can contract a disease and ignore the symptoms. Learn your body. If you develop a rash, blister, irritation, discharge, bleeding, etc., get examined immediately by a professional. I am no expert on diseases, I'm aware of what I've learned throughout my life that I believe may be helpful to women.

Here's a few of the diseases listed online by the Center for Disease Control that women can contract from men:

> **HIV** – Human Immunodeficiency Virus is not AIDS but can lead to an HIV positive person developing AIDS. If you have syphilis, herpes, or gonorrhea, you may be more prone to getting HIV, based on sexual behavior, or a break in your skin such as a blister, rash, or tear caused from friction, waxing, or shaving. Once you contract HIV, it's in your body forever. There's a drug (you can take daily) to help prevent getting HIV-1, if you are HIV negative. It's Truvada for PrEP (pre-exposure prophylaxis). There's also treatment, antiretroviral therapy (ART). People who get treatment early may never develop AIDS.
> **AIDS** – Acquired Immunodeficiency Syndrome is an advanced stage of infection from HIV that

makes is extremely difficult for your body's immune system to function properly. A CD4 cell count of less than 200, in an HIV-infected person, results in an AIDS diagnosis. A basic cold can turn into pneumonia in a person with AIDS.

HPV – Human Papillomavirus Virus is most commonly transferred during vaginal and anal sex, but also can be spread during oral sex even when the person has no signs. This is scary but there are other viruses with no symptoms. Often ladies, you won't know you or your partner has it. Best case scenario, it can go away on its own. Worse case, it can develop into cervical cancer.

BV – Bacterial Vaginosis is an imbalance of "good" and "harmful" bacteria in the vagina. Having a new sex partner, multiple sex partners, or douching can throw off your bacterial balance. I suggest women douche only when necessary. If you think you have a yeast infection, get over the counter medication. A man's penis has germs. I know some women are in protection-free relationships. Showering before sex is a good thing. Make sure to rinse off soaps and body washes well. Ladies, how many times has a guy not washed his ass, dick, balls, or hands before penetrating your vagina? His entire body is full of bacteria that may be harmful to your vagina. You may develop itching and irritation or BV. Cleanliness before intercourse is essential. When possible, don't let him skip showering.

HSV – Herpes Simplex Type 1 (oral) and Herpes Simplex Type 2 (genital) is extremely common. One out of every six person (in the United States) between the ages of 14 and 49, have genital herpes. Most don't know it because they've never been tested for genital herpes. Type 1 can be spread to the genital area if oral sex is performed during the onset of a breakout on the lips, or if a lip blister still has fluid. An intimate kiss followed by genital contact may infect you or your lover. I imagine the spread of this disease is larger in part to a lack of education. Some people spread Type 1 to their genital from touching the blister on their lip, not washing their hands before touching their vagina (maybe after urination) or penis (during urination). Most people wash their hands after using the restroom. A better practice is to wash your hands before and after.

Some other diseases to self-educate yourself on are:

Chlamydia
Gonorrhea
Hepatitis
Syphilis
Trichomoniasis
PD – Pelvic Inflammatory Disease

In my *Head Master* class, I teach fellatio and cunnilingus techniques. I teach women who don't want to engage in oral

Dicks are Dumb

sex or intercourse, how to give a man an amazing hand job. Why? Because men don't care how they cum as long as they cum and sometimes a woman does not want a man ejaculating inside of any parts of her, but she cares enough to please him.

For me, it's not about the guy's satisfaction. Before I take off my panties, I need to feel that he possesses the knowledge and skills to please me. Too many women are sexually frustrated. Men don't care about your satisfaction, ladies. How many times has a man cum, then fell asleep or left you?

If I detect that a man is a selfish lover, not good in bed, has lazy mannerisms, is disrespectful, doesn't wash his hands and/or his dick, I couldn't care less about how much he wants me, I don't want him touching me. There are lots of ways to tell, ladies. Start by listening and being attentive to what he says and does. Undereducated men hate to be quizzed on the female anatomy. That dumb dick just wants to fuck and he's so dumb you can't teach his ass any new tricks.

Speaking of tricks, a lot of men are intimidated by women who enjoy sex. What they will do is pay close attention to everything she does (or tells him). He's too insecure to try anything with her that she's taught him, but he'll try all of what she's shown him with the next female, to impress her. Men are not smarter than women.

The first person a woman needs to stop judging when it comes to sex is herself. Eliminate your self-guilt. Even if you're married or believe in monogamy, give yourself permission to explore your sexuality. You might surprise yourself.

HoneyBHonest: It's your pussy, not his!

Recommended Reading:
Nothing Has Ever Felt Like This by Mary B. Morrison

10
Every Dick Has a Dumb Moment

Chastising a grown man down the block and around the corner for cheating is a waste of your time ladies. Evaluate what transpired, decide how you want to handle the situation, then move forward.

All dicks plead the fifth because they believe women are stupid enough to believe whatever lie they concoct. When caught, if your guy cares about you he'll claim it wasn't him (even if you saw him), tell you the woman doesn't mean shit to him, defame the woman he sexed convincing you she's a whore, lie and say he only had sex with her once when he's fucking her on the regular, blame you for withholding sex, promise not to do it again when the truth is he can't wait to hit that pussy again, say there's no way the baby is his and tell you he used protection when he's never used a condom with any of his extras. But the one thing the dick does not do is deny it's had…a dumb dick moment.

HoneyBHonest: Most men would fail a lie detector test when it cums to infidelity.

If your guy outright tells you to your face, yes, I fucked her, he does not care about you at all. It's backward, I know but dumb dicks lie to the women they love. Men can and do fall in-love with more than one woman at the same time. He wants ownership of all his pussies. Sometimes the man falls in-lust with the other woman because he can do with her what he doesn't do sexually with his woman/wife. She's his go-to gurl.

When a man has idle time, he's thinking about sex. There are times where he's out with his friends (or solo) not focusing on getting off, then along comes a woman and sits beside him. Automatically, his dick wants to say hello. Your man may truly struggle to avoid communicating with her but temptation dicktates that there's no harm in being polite. In the first ten to fifteen minutes, if your man wants to do the right thing, he will reference you by saying my woman, my girlfriend, or my wife to let the woman know he's unavailable. He's not necessarily disinterested. He's trying to do the right thing. Your man's acknowledgement of you does not mean his dick does not become aroused by deliciousness and his dick can convince the ego there's no harm in saving the woman's number in his phone.

He locks in Brenda as Barry and Jessica as Home Depot to outsmart his inquisitive woman. Then he selects 'block caller' knowing voicemail messages will still register if she leaves one. Your man may secure a Google number that transcribes a voicemail message to an email that goes to an address that his gurl doesn't know exist. There may be a second cell that you've never seen where he only checks the voicemail as desired. He also deletes the cell number from the call log of the cell he leaves unlocked and gives you total access to. Oh, where there's a will, he'll find his way. And women who think their man is transparent, he's smarter than his dick.

Don't worry ladies. There's no need to search the cookies on his computer or place a tracking device on his phone or car.

Stop wasting your precious pussy time spying on your man. Do, you! My dad said, if you're searching for something, you'll find it. Then what? Maybe you confront your man but then you become the one with trust issues. No matter how hard your man tries to outthink you, his dumb dick will eventually slip up.

HoneyBHonest: Keep your man meaningfully engaged before and well after the honeymoon.

Men enjoy watching porn, often. They watch reality television to check out the females' tits and ass, the drama is lagniappe (extra). Guys are guilty of sexting and texting multiple women back-to-back (with the same message) hoping at least one of them will agree to do him. This could happen when he's out on a date with you.

Facetime is perfect for cybersex and you may be asleep in the bed next to him while he's jacking off. If he's in a relationship Netflix and Chill with his extras is preferred for several reasons. One, all he really wants to do is fuck. Two, he's not trying to waste money on taking her easy ass out. Three, being in public is risky as his woman, her girlfriends, or someone else that knows them will catch him creeping. A pic or video could pop up on his woman's cell in less than a minute.

His dick doesn't care if he's caught. The lie he'd have to create is a headache that his dick doesn't have to deal with when he gets home sweet home to the main.

Jacking off, thumbing through naked magazines, going through his phone to see if he can get lucky, is all about his dick, not him. Men also DM females, and replay unforgettable sexcapades in their mind while fucking their wife.

If the dick has not voluntarily totally detached from the ex, men continue communicating with the same woman well after they get caught and occasionally, puts a ring on her, whereas he's never given a ring to the main. That's a dumb dick moment.

HoneyBHonest: Ladies, never forget. A dick has a head but it doesn't have a brain.

There's not one man that I've asked if he's had a dumb dick moment that has replied, no. Very few dumb dicks have regrets. In fact, cheating is often more pleasurable and memorable than being faithful. The dick can't remember what it did. Only knows what it wants to do next. Notice I said what, not whom.

HoneyBHonest: Smart dicks don't exist. Intelligent and successful men do.

Good dick isn't hard to cum by when women know how to judge a man before he pulls that thang out. The challenge for lots of women is being intimate first, then expecting the dick to give a fuck about them after it cums.

HoneyBHonest: Character flaws are rooted in a man's dick.

Sex is amazing! Like Samantha on, *Sex In The City*, HoneyB loves to enjoy a man. Ladies take your time determining if he's worthy of penetrating you. Be comfortable exercising your options. Do not feel obligated to do him under any cir-cum-stances. The ultimate choice and responsibility is incumbent upon the woman.

HoneyBHonest: Dicks do not accept responsibility for a man's actions.

Lots of men will not stroke your nipples, caress your breasts, or kiss your clit. He even finger fucks like a maniac. Don't let a dumb dick jab you in your good pussy like he's a light or heavyweight in round ten.

Conversations matter.

Watch out for the narcissist. His love of self leaves no room for him to love anyone else. He dominates the conversation.

Inhales, holds his breath, waits for you to pause, then redirects the topic back to himself. No matter what you say, he has a story or comment that relates to him. Everything revolves around this guy. Realize that you can't change his point of view. And his dumb dick is on an axel that revolves around him.

Be cognizant of how much he cares about getting to know you, while his clothes are on. Some guys say what they think you want to hear in order to cum inside of you. Comments are not inquiries. You've heard guys that have a long list of compliments. He says, you're so cute. You're so fine. I can't believe you're single. At the end of this type of dialogue, he still doesn't know much about you. Ladies, need to learn to listen, ask questions, take notes, and trust your instincts, especially during your first few conversations with a man. Ladies, the don't ask, don't tell applies to this guy.

Mannerisms matter.
Sloppy eater. Sloppy lover. That's not to say you want a neat freak feasting between your thighs, but you definitely don't want him trying to suction out your ovaries or as a friend told me "he attacks the clit". He's a dumb ass dick, and he has a black belt in karate. What a man does for a living often translates to how he makes love. A mechanic, sanitation worker, lawyer, doctor, are all different. Often musicians are the absolute best lovers because they understand the importance of being in-tune with a woman as they would their instruments. Plus, they have an ear for sounds. Some men are extremely heavy handed. If you like it rough, he might be your guy, but keep in mind when choosing your dick, an attentive man with a caring touch is probably a good lover.

Size matters?

Not as much as most women think. The average size non-African-American man's penis is 5.6 inches. The average size African-American man's penis is 6.5 inches.

What's really important when it comes to a dick?

Strong PC muscles create a firm foundation that contribute significantly to good stamina and penetration. Hitting the gym is cool as long as he's including lots of squats for the inner thighs. But most men don't believe they need to do Kegels. They do. Out of ignorance, men think Kegels are for women only. A man's muscles weaken as he gets older, making it increasingly difficult for him to penetrate a woman. If he's on medication, the meds can contribute to his being flaccid. The bigger his dick, the larger his problem. Women appreciate sexy hard bodies. If a woman has to choose, I know a significant number would prefer that her man has the ability to please her sexually no matter his size.

Can you imagine never getting a tune-up on brand new car? When a man has to yank, tug, slap, jerk his dick to make it hard, size won't save him from embarrassment. This man has a dumb dick that's determined to cum and he couldn't care less if he pleases the woman. Men need to exercise (tune-up) their dick to help prevent erectile dickfunction.

More men are having ED moments at earlier ages because they believe ejaculating all the time is good for them but it's the opposite. Imagine if a man would only get one new set of tires for the lifetime of his vehicle. Would he drive recklessly? Probably not. Well, he's only going to have one dick. A smart man will not wear his dick out with random fucks. But the average man will.

Ladies do not want a fish dick. Imagine holding a fish by its tail, then picture trying to shove the head into crushed ice. No woman wants a dick slipping, bending, and flopping like a dead fish when she's hot and ready for great sex.

If a woman opens her legs for a man that has a limp dick, he'll say, she's too tight, too dry, or she need to relax. A dumb dick will make his inability to perform the woman's fault. Ladies are never to blame for a man's dick's problems.

Hygiene Matters.
A dumb dick doesn't care if it's clean. The head of his penis is sandwiched between his balls and his asshole all day long. Some guys shake, shake, shake after urinating, then tuck the head in without cleaning it off. Others swipe and go after defecating. Hint the skid mark in the underwear. This same guy will take his dirty dick and penetrate a woman's good pussy. That's truly a dumb dick moment when a man puts a woman at-risk for an infection.

Ladies, it's okay to insist that a guy clean his genitals before having sex with him.

There's a difference between sweaty and filthy. Musky and musty. Do not put a dirty dick in your mouth or vagina.

Recommended Reading: *W hen Somebody Loves You Back* by Mary B. Morrison

IV

Whose Team is His Dick On

11
He's Bi-Sexual

Men who like penetration don't necessarily want it from another man.

What's wrong with a man partaking in sexual pleasure with women and men?

Pause for a moment. Are you who you want to be? Or, are you the person others expect you to be? Whatever your response is, please understand the answers are deeply rooted in who you are. A lot of individuals are bold enough to live their own truth but they derive a false sense of satisfaction from condemning others.

Bi-sexual men lie more than homosexual men out of fear of being dehumanized, and rejected by women, not men. You're entitled to your opinion, we all are, but your feelings have absolutely nothing to do with a person's sexual desires. Equally, the negative words people speak of you only matter if it bothers you.

HoneyBHonest: People who hate are hurting inside.

There's a vast difference between hating someone, especially a person you don't have a relationship with, as opposed to being angry with an individual that has violated you. It's best to live and let live.

Ladies, would you date an openly bi-sexual male? I ask, as quite a few women are in situations with men who are secretly sexing men. It's troubling that these men are deceitful. Men lie to get laid. Men lie to be loved, by women.

Women don't have to buy into a man's ridickulousness. If you find out he's bi-sexual, and you find it repulsive, bitching won't convert him. There's no need to argue, ladies. Move on!

I know some females are in relationships where the guy is a great father, awesome husband, and your best friend. If he's into men, you may want to establish an agreement. Maybe you stop being intimate, agree to have an open relationship but not have sex with one another. If dick is all he's bringing, let him go.

The number of men (single and married) having intercourse with men and women is on the rise. I have yet to read a dating book written by a man that seriously addresses one of the biggest concerns for women. Is he bi-sexual? How can I tell? Most of the time, you can't because your man is a liar and manipulator.

Honesty does not offend me as long as a man is respectful. I've been in bed with men who flip onto their back, raise their knees beside their ears, and submit their asshole to me. I've been asked to strap-on, make love, grind like I was the dude but without a dildo. Some men act as though they're the female, but they don't want to be with a man.

Clearly, these types of guys would be repulsive to most women. Not me. This goes to people knowing what they want. If I invite a man into my bedroom, I've assessed he's a good lover, and I'm very accommodating. How could I write about sex if I were a prude?

In a more detailed situation, I was showering with a fine ass man. I squeezed body wash into my palm, then slid my hand between his butt cheeks. Instantaneously, he leaned against the tiles and moaned repeatedly. The more I stroked his rectum, the louder he grunted. I was like, damn all this dick and I'll never know how it feels inside of me. He was approximately 10 ½ inches with massive girth. I wasn't sure he'd fit but before that first moan, I was willing to try. We didn't have intercourse nor did we do oral. I appreciated that he was open so I got the coconut oil and treated him to an amazing hand job. He contacted me later asking if I could get him one of the sex dolls I had on the bar in my house. I told him, of course.

Men in power don't always want to be in control, often they welcome being dominated in the bedroom but don't want to ask a woman for anal stimulation fearing she'll not just think but also call him gay. I share these experiences because I don't judge what men like.

I like exploring slipping a finger into his orbit while driving him insane with oral. By the time he climaxes, he's wondering how to ask the next woman to pleasure him in a similar fashion. He can practically forget about it. Sexually uninhibited women are sparse. But gay men willing to sex straight men are plentiful.

I don't like women or men to deny or suppress their sexual spirit.

HoneyBHonest: If you live a lie, you attract a liar.

A wealthy African guy was open enough to ask if I had a strap-on. I was in Houston and my strap-on was at home in Oakland but I promised myself never to cross the state line of Texas again without a harness and dildo in my suitcase. He wined and dined me in five-star fashion. We're still cool with one another.

Each of these men denied being bi-sexual. One is married, one is in a long-term committed relationship, the other guy is a popular DJ, and the last one is an entrepreneur who travels Internationally. Based on what I know, I'd say all of them are try-sexual.

HoneyBHonest: We can't put a limit on the complexities of sexuality.

I believe that up to seventy-two gender identifications are documented. I can't keep up with each classification. What I do know is, no matter how many times a woman asks her guy if he's had sex, or thought about having sex with a man, he's not confessing. It's like inquiring if he's ever raped, molested, or beaten a girl, boy, man or woman. He'll lie before pleading the fifth because in this case, saying nothing, is presumed to be a "yes".

Of the long list of derogatory names society has labeled people with, being bi-sexual is not a title a bi-sexual man will claim. Have you ever met a guy who has said, hello, my name is Tom and I'm bi-sexual? The second a man says that, social epithets dicktates he's gay.

Bi-sexual and gay are not the same. It's like trying to justify yellow and purple are the same colors; or stating that there's no difference between a one and a one-hundred-dollar bill. The down side of the down low is ignorant, judgmental, lying, cheating men who believe a man's sexuality defines his manhood. Every woman should have at least one gay bestie. I'm a good judge of dicks, but sometimes even I need a second look.

HoneyBHonest: Dumb dicks are to blame for the pain and suffering in the majority of relationships because dicks lie without having a conscious.

Undercover gay men (pastors included) bash openly gay men in order to hide what they're doing. Men sexually abuse then degrade women to mask their insecurities. Men manipulate women, then emotionally sabotage the very same women they ejaculated inside of.

A number of gay men have told me how so-called straight and married men pursue them all the time. One openly gay man showed me a sex video of a married man (with two daughters). As I watched this attractive married man with an amazing athletic build thrusting his dick fast and hard, in and out, grinding into the gay guy's rectum, Mr. Family Man was not wearing protection when he pulled out and shot cum all over the opening of the gay guy's asshole. Ladies, can you imagine that being your man? It might be.

The saddest part was the gay guy is HIV positive and the married man is clueless. That wasn't their first time having intercourse raw and probably wouldn't be their last.

This is why I say, "Fuck all those relationship books telling women to act like a fucking lady, when they should be reading *Dicks are Dumb*.

Honesty and safe sex could decrease the number of women infected with a sexually transmitted disease by bi-sexual and other men who cheat and don't wear condoms.

When I vacation where adults unite with the intentions of fucking strangers, I'm not on penis or pussy patrol, I'm the condom and lube diva passing out complimentary gold and blue packets. A lot of people don't know that the anus does not produce lubrication. When I tell guys that, they quickly add a few tubes of lube to their stash. Actually, people thank me and I feel like maybe, just maybe, I've helped to prevent the spread of disease.

When I approached one couple, the guy took several condoms. The female snatched his wrist declaring he didn't need any, then demanded he put them back. After a little Q&A, I learned they'd just hooked up at the resort. I insisted he keep them, gave him a few more, then side-eyed that crazy bitch for discouraging a man from doing the right thing. Minutes later, he was in another woman's face flirting while the chick he'd abandoned was sour-faced in her seat waiting on him to return. Bitch, he's only coming back to pussy-on-pause if the other woman (who's clearly his preferred) turns him down.

Which reminds me, earlier that night, I ran into a dude I'd smashed years before. We were enjoying cocktails with one of his boyz. An openly gay man approached my friend, greeted him only, then left. I side-eyed my friend, then said, you're bisexual. I wasn't asking. Instantly, I saw it. And it was cool.

Just like men, too many women are in denial. Women are convinced. *Not my husband. Not my man. He'd never cheat. He's not sexing men. I don't need protection. I'm good. I don't have an STD.* Yes, your significant other can contract a sexually transmitted disease if he's having unprotected sex and he can transmit it to you—his woman. Problem is, most men think a woman is disease free because she looks, dresses, and carries herself in an impressionable manner. Tainted pussy is pretty. But how does she get that way?

Don't be quick to conclude your spouse is cheating. Sometime a man is being faithful and he transmits a disease. The same can happen with women as well. For example, a man with a penile prosthesis can carry bacteria that can transmit trichomoniasis to his woman. A woman can develop a yeast infection from certain medications and transmit the yeast infection to her man.

I recall contracting a yeast infection from using my girlfriend's bath towel after her. It was the only one she had.

The towel was moist. I dried off, including between my legs. Later I started itching. Went to the doctor and sure enough, the doctor said I could've gotten it because bacteria can survive in damp places. The same is true for herpes. I never did that again.

In some cases, people are accusing their mate of infidelity when their mate hasn't cheated at all. Again, ignorance is the root of a lot of people's misery and insecurity. Knowing your health status and your body helps tremendously.

HoneyBHonest: When you don't trust yourself, it's impossible to trust others.

Men fear going to the doctor due to the dreaded finger up the butt and cough exam. Truth is, a rectal, prostate and colon exam can save a man's life. The more men know about their overall health, the more they may want to ensure they protect their dick. Maybe.

A woman will verbally (and sometimes physically) abuse her husband's female lover until the DNA comes back 99.99999 percent that her husband is the father. Then a woman will side with her husband against the mother of his child. Then she learns her man is having sex with men too.

A woman is never to blame for her man cheating.

Having a child outside of a relationship is problematic but it's not as complicated as the individual that perpetuates the lies of infidelity. I pray one day the women who give their man the benefit of the doubt (over the mistress/side), get the facts first, then respond accordingly.

HoneyBHonest: Sometimes a man is truthful. Often, he's the one lying.

It's okay for a man to be bi-sexual. It's not okay for him to deceive women.

Dicks are Dumb

Here's what I think is sheer bananas. If a woman discovers her man is sexing men, she gets mad with her husband. If she finds out he has a side chick, she relentlessly blames the female.

HoneyBHonest: Men have truly got women brainwashed.

Bi-sexual men will not always be honest and the truth is, some of them would rather be committed to a man. But what would his mother, father, sister, brother, cousin, co-workers, friends, pastor, and wife think of him falling in-love with a man? I know men who have divorced their wife then married a man.

The only reason double-standards thrive is—like a game of follow the leader—women support the foolishness. Women need to stop chasing men! Think. And live for themselves.

Guys say it's a turn on to watch two women have sex. It's natural for men to have more than one sex partner. Even if he's married, he's forgiven for his indiscretions. He can stay out all night or come home whenever he wants. His woman has to ask him to babysit their kids. Fuck that!

I set the tone early in my marriage. Before we were pregnant, I cooked and he ironed our clothes. When I returned to work from maternity leave, my then husband and I, shared responsibilities for every household responsibility. One week I woke up in the middle of the night to care for our child, the next week, he did it all – from changing diapers, to dressing, bathing, to getting up in the middle of the night to feed our child— he did it all. And, he enjoyed the experience.

HoneyBHonest: Women need to relax and let men participate in the relationship.

A man (even if he's bi-sexual) can leave a woman and his kids and get another woman the same day. Doing it all does not keep a man at home or make him faithful.

In reality, women could move on quickly too, if they weren't weak minded when it came to men. Women sit around hoping a man she didn't like in the first damn place comes back to her. Let that bitch ass dude step. She probably had a doll growing up. Stop giving little girls baby dolls.

Most men can't count the number of vaginas they've penetrated. Is it irrelevant? Absolutely. On both ends. Ladies, never tell a man how many lovers you've had. I don't care if it's two or two thousand and two. Your past is not his fucking business. If he asks, do like I do— ask him, how many men have you been with?

Men prejudge women all the time. I don't care what men think of me. It's simple. You like me or you don't. I like you, or I don't.

HoneyBHonest: It's easy to strip a man of having power over you because the only power he has is the power you give him.

Before you encounter a bisexual man, a few things occur. One, most women never ask the question, "Are you bisexual?" Women assume the man must be straight if he's interested in her. Ask the damn question, ladies! Whether he laughs or becomes defensive, his canned lies are already scripted. A man will take a lie in two directions. One, to the altar. Two, to his grave. Just because he stands at the altar, puts a ring on your finger, and is the father of your children, pussy does not make him heterosexual.

How can you tell if your man enjoys sex with men?

If he tells you, which he probably won't. If you catch him in the act, which he'll still deny the truth. If another man makes an advance toward your guy in front of you, and your man suddenly has to use the restroom, you might want to side-eye him when he gets back to the table.

If a man is open to everything, he'll try anything. If your man's dick gets hard watching another man he's attracted to men.

Most importantly ladies, trust your instincts. Not your judgment.

Recommended Reading: *Single Husbands* by HoneyB

12
Sex Behind Bars

If a man goes to jail for rape, word is he's going to get raped. Repeatedly. I've heard child molesters are treated worse. That's great! Dumb ass dicks don't deserve to get off at all.

If every man that has raped and/or molested a girl or woman were convicted, dudes behind bars would get tired of raping rapists. When will men understand that no means, no? A lot of men in relationship believe it's a woman's obligation to have sex whenever he wants to and if he forces her, it's his right. It's not!

I was talking to a thirty-year-old male friend. He said, in order for him to be faithful, his woman/wife must never deny his sexual advances no matter where they are. If she does, then he's going to cheat.

Let's keep it real. I told him, you're going to cheat regardless. That's your fucking excuse. If you have that stipulation on your relationship, you're prepared to justify cheating on her. Men like him need variety, and no matter how accommodating his woman is, eventually he'll get bored. If he raped her, she told the police, and he went to jail, he'd blame her. But that's exactly what should happen. Let him experience what it feels like to have a dick shoved inside of him.

Dicks are Dumb

A man may not be satisfied with jacking off all time when he's locked up, especially if he's sentenced to life. Life does not mean he'll never get out but it's a long time to be behind bars. Some won't hesitate to accept a blowjob, or perhaps engage in anal sex with a man. The majority of these men will never claim they're gay, never admit they've fucked or have been fucked or raped by a man.

It could be true that he does not and has never had the desire to have sex with a man. People adapt to their environment. My military guy friend said he did not see a woman for eighteen months while stationed in Afghanistan. I found that hard to imagine. Wow. I'd never thought of what life would be like if we never saw the opposite sex for over a year. He said, he'd never had sex with a man. That could've been true, but would a straight man voluntarily admit he allow his dick to enter any part of a man?

There are reported cases where female prison guards have been impregnated by men who are incarcerated. He has nothing to lose, so why do his best convincing her to let him fuck her. She has a lot to lose starting with her job. Her problem, not his. He just wants to fuck and if he can cum inside of a pussy, he'll say whatever it takes.

It's not much on the outside. A man will lie and beg to get laid.

Inmates in certain situations are allowed to receive visits, some conjugal. More than likely, he has not been tested for STDs, and may have had with a man behind bar, but it doesn't matter. He's not turning down pussy.

HoneyBHonest: There are some men who will not engage in sexual contact with a man regardless of his circumstances.

Getting raped (in or out of prison) doesn't make a man gay. There are men out there sticking their dick in the mouths and assholes of little boys and teenagers. From pissing to ejaculating there are a lot of dumb ass dicks. Most men get away with raping women and children (boys are molested too) because rape is the one crime that authorities make the victim feel as though they are the fucking culprit.

Rape kits by the thousands are never tested. Rapists are seldom convicted. At the end of a trial, the female or male feels shamed and stupid for even trying to get justice. Her interaction with every man she's had sex with can be brought into question. Yet, the man's past is seldom the focus because he can't be tried for crimes he's not charged with. If he gets off, he's comfortable raping again.

I'm not sure of all of what happened in the Bill Cosby case, but the details which were mentioned, disgusted me to the point of wanting to throw up! I wished he would've been sentenced to life and died behind bars.

I have zero compassion for rapists.

Being behind bars does not diminish a man's urge to have sex. He wants to cum. He has to cum. And for most men incarcerated, at some point they will be released.

Ladies, be aware. Every good-looking man does not have your best interest at heart. A lot of guys in jail are communicating with as many women as they can, lying to each one as he professes his love. He wouldn't marry her when he was a free man, but now that he's locked up his ass is proposing.

Women are holding these guys down, but when they get out, they want a divorce. Remember that convict, turned super model who allegedly left his family for a rich woman?

I say, "A man too fine, has probably done time." Background check the man/men you're interested in dating, ladies.

I went out with a guy who was evasive about where he lived and if he was in a relationship. My gut instincts said run a report on him. I did. His record showed multiple arrests for battery, domestic violence and assault. I emailed him the report asking if that were him, to see what he'd say. I knew it was him.

This is the kind of shit men who write relationship books don't fucking mention to women.

He was extremely upset, and told me, "I didn't give you permission to do a background check on me."

I let him know, I didn't need his permission. You don't either ladies. Check his ass out! All kinds of information is available online and if you can't find him online, don't fuck with him.

HoneyBHonest? Men are going to get laid wherever they lay their heads.

Recommended Reading: *Sexcapades* by HoneyB

13
He Doesn't Know

That's a lie! A man definitely knows which team his dick is on.

He may struggle with acceptance of his desires to be with a man, or coming out if he's gay, but a man knows who he wants to have sex with.

Unfortunately, the world is full of unnecessary hate and haters who derive pleasure from condemning others. Maybe one day we will live in a society free of judgment and condemnation for freedom of sexuality.

HoneyBHonest: If you cannot stand in your own truth, you don't respect yourself or others. It's a character flaw to believe you're honest, if every day you open your eyes you're living a lie. Women shouldn't have to wonder if the man penetrating her is doing the same with men.

Every woman needs a gay best friend to help her determine if her new man is straight. Can gay men always tell if another man is gay. No. Almost always? Yes.

If a man is suspect, and I like him enough to commit to a relationship with him, I invite my fabulous gay crew to tell me the truth. I'll meet my guy at a bar, ask a gay friend to come by and act like we just ran into one another. Then I'll introduce my guy to my friend and chat for a few minutes. When my friend leaves, he'll text me his thoughts.

One time I invited one of my male lovers to a gay restaurant where my gay friend was a waiter. I told my guy exactly where we were dining before we got there. Full disclosure here. No surprises. I dined at the bar with my guy, who is extremely fit and handsome. Perfect white teeth. Muscles all over his body. Flat abs. Buns of steel. All that. My guy was totally comfortable. Several men hit on him but my guy did not respond to any of them. Even the bartender talked to my guy as if I weren't seated in the next stool.

My gay friend confirmed, your guy is not gay. He said, one, a bi-sexual man is not knowingly going to a gay restaurant in fear of the fact that he might see an ex-lover. Two, a bi-sexual man in a predominantly gay environment will pretend he's appalled by gay men fearing the woman may pick up on his attraction to men.

Out of all the horrible things men have done to women, very few men ask or care whether or not a woman has experienced sexual trauma.

HoneyBHonest: Women need to, without shame or guilt, let men know the abuse done to them by other men.

Recommended Reading:
Maneater by Mary B. Morrison and Noire

14
Stop Dying for His Dick

Is he worth dying for? Seriously?
Why do women go crazy over dick when all dicks are emotionally unavailable?

A dumb dick can kill you in many ways, including murder. Men who kill their spouse receive an average sentence of two to six years. Ninety percent of women who kill their spouse were victims of physical abuse and get an average sentence of fifteen years. You may be wondering why the huge difference in years. Men usually strangle or beat their woman to death. Women generally use a weapon. When a man kills with his hands, his hands should be declared a lethal weapon.

I have to touch on subject matters that male writers opt to skip because some shit seems cool in theory, but mentally unstable men are real. And many of them appear sane in the beginning. A woman may not technically be in a relationship with a man, and out the gate he's putting her down or maybe stalking her. Take your time getting to know a man, ladies. I suggest the first time he beats you, leave his stupid angry ass alone!

Choose your dick wisely. Do the math ladies, and don't be so quick to share your good pussy. You do not have to impress him. That's his responsibility. A woman never has to fight for a man who loves her. Truth is, most women scream, curse, cry, and some assault the other woman because they are afraid of losing what they've never had—the man. Shit might seem cute at the time— all that "for my man" crap, but if you end up behind bars boxing every damn day (possibly getting your ass whupped) to survive while he moves on to the next female, you'll probably feel like a damn fool.

Bad dick can change a woman's life...forever.

I keep saying, and it's real—it's important for women to know what they want from a man before engaging in sexual activity. I hear men say, "I told her I didn't want a relationship. She agreed. Said she could handle that". Then he grins when the woman gets jealous of other females and starts stalking his ass. You become his clown, not a class act.

A friend told me after he dicks a woman down really well, he has nothing but problems. Women drive by his house all times of the day to see if another woman is there. They relentlessly text and call him. But I know this guy. He's financially well off and spends money on his dates. He's a gentleman. He admits that the women who chase him stroke his ego. He was so busy fucking over females that when a one he fell in love with didn't fall for his bullshit, he regretted treating her like the rest. She left him permanently.

HoneyBHonest: When the head games go too far, good guys kill women too.

Ladies, you are a fucking speck and spectacle in some of these guys' eyes. He strokes his ego while telling his boy how much of fool you are. He's the fuckboy!

Ladies, you have to separate the man from the fuck buddy from the fuckboy.

The man gives a fuck. The buddy just wants to fuck. And the fuckboy intentionally fucks over you. Some men make women want to kill them. You can't convince the jester that dating is not a joke.

What do you want, ladies? Stop catching feelings when you barely know a guy.

It's virtually impossible for a woman to be a sex buddy for an extended period of time and not want a commitment from the man she's sexing. When a man penetrates a woman, he ejaculates/transfers his energy into her body. This is why it's best to know what you want ladies before he cums. Can you change your mind during the act of intercourse? Absolutely. Will a man change his mind about how he views his relationship with you if you leave him hanging? If he's in it for the pussy, yes. If he's into you, no.

No one wants to feel used, but men are users. They're also disillusioned. They don't accept responsibility for their actions no matter how much they destroy the people around them, their children included. Lots of men are minimalists. It's easier for men to lean on women than for them to depend upon themselves.

Trust me, I know this is not true for every man but too many guys blame women for their shortcomings and their shortcumings.

Women are constantly struggling to find a good and faithful man but ladies you don't have to die to have dick. Survival of the fittest is in your favor if you learn how to utilize sex to your advantage.

This may require a period of celibacy , even if you're in a relationship. I'm not suggesting six months to a year, although lots of women have been celibate for much longer.

Dicks are Dumb

Try to learn something new about the man you're interested in each time you speak with him. First, middle, and last names. Address. Family. Friends. Occupation. Goals. Relationship values. Views on sex and women. How does he feel about kids? Yours. His. Having children. Perhaps you're the one who doesn't want to have a baby. Is he okay with that?

Men are meant to enjoy, not stress over.

Let a man pay for at least the first three dates. By then, you should know if you want to be intimate with him. Often, when a woman dives into sex right away (first date) she finds herself chasing the man like she can get her pussy back. It's totally acceptable for a woman to have sex on the first date, but she must be clear on why she's doing it. Take ownership of the decision, not the dick. Remember, the dick doesn't have a brain.

HoneyBHonest: Always let a man like and love you more.

When a woman chases a guy, she's desperate. He knows you'll do just about anything to have him. Unless he can see where you're of benefit to him, he's looking for someone better than you.

Every day women destroy themselves emotionally and physically over dick, including dumb dicks. Women plead for men that don't deserve them. Ladies cry themselves to sleep. You drive yourself insane worrying about the other woman he's with or if he's with another woman. All this and more deteriorates your overall health causing you to lose or gain weight, neglect your family, friends, children, and yourself.

While a woman suffers (often in silence), the man moves on with his life, as she prays one day, one day, one day, he'll come back to her and make her happy. She dreams that he'll accept her and his children and make them a whole family. A text, a

DM, or a call, he knows, gives her hopeless hope and keeps her clinging to him.

Men love to mislead women. Their egos are equally as dumb as their dick because he's happy to see her sad. This is why as long as a woman is dying to be with him, he's good. The second she moves on, gets a new man, and she's happy without him, the dumb dick goes on a mission to destroy her happiness because he's not the one bringing her joy and he envisions the other man's dick is pleasing what he considers to still be his pussy.

HoneyBHonest: A man can never offer a woman what he does not possess.

If he does not value loyalty, commitment, respect, etc., what does he have to give a woman? Dick.

My son and his fiancée, during their engagement (they're married now), abstained from having sex for a year before saying, I do, in order to get to know one another at their most intimate and vulnerable state. How many couples can honestly say they have invested quality time in one another? A lot of couples are in sexless situations.

If a person outside of your relationship knows your partner better than you (including your best friend), you have a lot to learn about your man.

I have to mention that some guys believe, if they can't have you, no one else will. Be careful to whom you give your heart to ladies. Every man does not have good intentions.

I dated a man that had a beautiful spirit plagued with demons. I'd witnessed him threaten to kill someone for cutting him off while driving. I was in his car with him when he tried to run other drivers off the road for driving too slow or if they were texting while driving he instantly became angry. Small things triggered his behavior. I told him we could not be together but I offered to help him get help through the Veterans Administration. He refused.

I saw him struggle to get better on his own. One day I awakened to find him standing over me staring down at me. He was so quiet I did not hear him come up the stairs. I freaked out. My reaction didn't faze him.

This same person taught me how never to touch a bullet without gloves. If shells don't have fingerprints on the casing, a crime cannot be traced back to me. He taught me how to leave a person for dead without injuring them. Outside of sports, all he wanted to watch was shows like *The First 48*.

He said if his mother ever died, he'd have nothing to live for. He has a daughter and family but this was a man that did not value life, not even his own.

Death is inevitable, but damn!

I say all of this to say, ladies, there are some men you cannot save from themselves, but they can snap and kill you. I thanked God that I didn't move in with him as he'd wanted. Yes, I left him, but to this day I pray for him.

Ladies, do not die or kill for a dumb ass dick.

Recommended Reading:
If I Can't Have You by Mary B. Morrison

V

The Diva and the Dick

15
Good Dick is Mandatory

Ladies, if you're not already, you need to pamper your pussy. I find most men are uncomfortable discussing sex. They just want to go zero to pussy. The reason they're hesitant is because most men are ignorant when it cums to how to please a woman.

Between the men who don't know what to do, don't care about a woman getting hers, have erectile dysfunction, have to take enhancement drugs and those who don't know how to perform cunnilingus, those are just some reasons why so many women have not experienced an orgasm. For the females that are multi-orgasmic, I imagine you know your body.

I hear the dumb dicks shouting, "It's her fault if she's never climaxed!" Wrong. I'm not going to rewrite the list of sexual crimes men commit, but those are contributing factors to the reasons some women are inhibited.

Women deserve to have gratifying sex.

Accept the fact that you are worthy of being romanced. Establish and express your expectations from a man pertaining to sex before you spread.

HoneyBHonest: Ladies, your vagina is no man's sperm bank.

Dicks are Dumb

Let's face the facts. Most men are not as good in bed as they could or should be. Guys get by with exerting very little effort. He wants you to get on top and wear yourself out until he's ready to ejaculate. Or he pumps fast and furious, cums, then he needs a recovery period. And don't let him be a premature ejaculator. Their stroke count may be three or less.

Seriously, I dated a "premie" shortly after my divorce. Nice guy. Took my son and I out to eat all the time. We vacationed together, once. Soon as he put the head in, he came and couldn't get it back up. I guess that was the point where I was supposed to think like a man and jack my shit.

No way in hell was I acting like a fucking lady. I did give him a second chance. Same thing happened. When I called him on his handicap, he got mad first, then he tried convincing me my good pussy was to blame. In the words of one of my favorite artists, I had to say, "Let's go kitty cat."

I know some females that stayed with guys just like my ex. I ask, "Why?" If you're clear why you stay, and you're happy, don't leave. If your pussy is depressed, you need a side dick.

Something about a man needs to turn you on before you take your clothes off.

Magnetic energy and undeniable chemistry can make a woman wet her panties in an instant. Our minds are so powerful, women can have touchless orgasms while awake, and climax in their sleep.

When you close your eyes at night, give yourself permission to visualize pleasure. Let the feeling permeate throughout your body. Take deep breaths until you doze off. I'm telling you woman are one step away from being asexual. It's a good thing we can't impregnate ourselves. Men wouldn't get any pussy.

Remember what I mentioned earlier. A woman's ass should never be wetter than her wallet.

Most men don't want to pay to cum. Men don't want to invest time in the women they cum inside of. Men are looking for easy and convenient women to lay, then he's on his way. Don't be that lady.

Tune in to your vagina. Is she excited? Is she tingling for the guy? Are your Bartholin glands leaking fluids? Does he make your breasts heave when you breathe? Do your eyes light up when you see him? Do you smile when his number registers on your caller I.D.?

Guys are quick to stick the head in without a brain into a woman's vagina. If she's dry, he blames her (out of his ignorance). The purpose of the Bartholin glands is to secrete mucous. This happens naturally when a woman is excited and her body wants to receive his manhood. If she's dry, it's because he either hasn't engaged her in foreplay, or her body is not stimulated by his advances.

Women need to listen to their body. Stop having sex with a man hoping he's going to become yours, or that he's going to pay your bills.

In current times, sometimes a woman just wants to grind and forget about him. I applaud women who are in touch with what they want. It's okay for a woman to fuck him where you find him, and leave him where you fuck him.

Yes, women can engage in sexual activities with the same attitude as men. Women are better equipped to have sex. Women do not suffer from erectile dickfunction. Women can increase their libido without enhancement drugs.

Ladies, remember when enhancement drugs hit the market for men and all these over the hill dudes were popping pills? Their dick was getting hard and staying that way. Some men were suffering heart attacks. Others couldn't afford the medication, so politicians found a way to grant access by making erectile dickfunction a disease.

Here's the real deal. No pill will make him a better lover. None. Men do not understand the complexities of the female anatomy. Men do not know how to sustain their sexual health or how to separate their orgasms from ejaculation. Men do not know how to pleasure the woman or engage in tantric sex.

Back to enhancement drugs— women don't need them. Remember, the commercials that used to promote sexual enhancement drugs for women. Remember, how those commercials slowly disappeared? When men suffer from anything sexually, they try to find a way to make women believe they have the same problem, or worse, that women are the problem.

Ladies, the power of the pussy is so dynamic that you can give yourself a mind-blowing orgasm without touching yourself. There are different ways to have a touchless orgasm. Ladies, you can mentally get aroused by a man and cum without ever taking your clothes off.

Here's a few ways to increase your libido or climax by yourself. Explore these ways. Virgins can do this as well, because having an orgasm does not require penetration or male stimulation. Welcoming a man into your womb has to be a conscious decision.

Lots of women are disconnected from their vagina. Let's work on changing that.

Breathing is key. Sit quietly or with soothing music playing.

1) Slowly inhale allowing your breasts to rise
2) Channel energy throughout your breasts
3) Inhale and exhale several times

4) When you inhale the fourth time, channel the energy throughout your breasts and to your nipples, as if someone is gently stroking or squeezing them
5) Allow yourself to be free of all judgment
6) Inhale into your belly and allow the energy to circulate in your womb
7) When you inhale for the sixth time let the energy flow to the opening of your vagina. Do not exhale yet
8) Act as though you're going to squeeze the opening/entry of your vagina but don't squeeze
9) Release the energy as if you're exhaling through your vagina
10) Repeat these steps as often as you like until you feel a connection with the powerful orgasmic energy inside of you.

The breathing exercise is wonderful for women who have never experienced having an orgasm. Some women can only climax from external stimulation. Others, only from anal penetration. But more often, this situation exists due to a disconnect with the vagina.

Here's another way to get closer to your pussy.

Kegels. Most women have heard of them. Few women actually do Kegels daily. You need to do your Kegels every day. After a week (if not sooner) you should notice a pleasant arousal (with or without a man). If you exercise daily, eventually during intercourse, when you climax, your man should feel your vaginal muscles throbbing along his head and shaft.

Dicks are Dumb

Here are instructions for performing Kegel exercises. Let's locate the correct muscles – the pubococcygeal (PC) muscles.

It's easy to contract the entire vulva. Kegels are about isolating the proper muscle. The best way to find the PC is during urination. The next time you urinate, squeeze and stop the flow of your urine. That's the correct muscle!

Now that you've found your PC, every time you urinate, squeeze and hold for three seconds to stop the flow. Do this at least three times. Each time you release, push. So what you're doing is squeezing, pushing, squeezing, pushing, squeezing and pushing. After the third time, relax until you're done.

You're not done yet. Actually, you're never done with Kegels. Let's take it up a notch. Literally. While watching television, listening to music, in a meeting, or while eating, you can do this. Find a time when your vaginal exercises will become spontaneous.

Inhale and squeeze your PC muscle, hold for three seconds, squeeze again, hold for three more seconds, but do not relax in between squeezing. Make each contraction tighter. After six seconds, exhale and relax. Start over with three seconds per squeeze, then gradually over days or weeks add another squeeze until you're squeezing up, up, and up until you cannot squeeze any higher.

HoneyBHonest: Good pussy is easy to find. A pussy that can learn tricks, is amazing!

Try this. Squeeze your PC muscle starting at the opening of your vagina. Squeeze up in a continual movement and don't stop until you can no longer tighten any higher. Hold for three seconds. Inhale while squeezing up. Exhale and relax. Be careful not to hold the muscle until you pass out.

Just for fun, and to illustrate how your vagina is connected to other parts of your body, open your eyes wide, now squint while your eyes are still wide open. Don't blink. You should feel your vagina slightly contract.

Think about climaxing. Be careful here. If you've been practicing you may surprise yourself and have an orgasm without touching yourself.

HoneyBHonest: Sex is 90% mental.

This is why most dicks don't know how to please you. Never forget that the dick does not have a brain. If you want to have mind-blowing sex ladies, you have to find a man that knows what he is doing.

For more fun, do your Kegels to the beat of your favorite music. I teach this in my vaginal aerobics class.

Make sure you purchase vaginal crystal eggs, a gem stone egg, and/or a crystal wand to elevate your Kegel exercises. You can insert the crystal wand while showering or brushing your teeth. Three to five minutes, once or twice a day is all you need. The eggs can be left in for hours. Your vaginal muscles should automatically retract around the crystals. This is perfect if you can't seem to remember to make time to exercise.

Consider exercising with your crystals and gems like working out at the gym with light weights. If you want to elevate more, you can purchase what's called a vaginal weight-lifting egg. This egg has a string secured at the tip of the egg. The string allows you to add additional weights (i.e., ¼ pound, ½ pound, 1 pounds, 5 pounds, and more). A woman's vaginal muscles are incredibly strong.

Get started exercising the next time you urinate.

The one thing good pussy does not tolerate is bad dick.

I was vacationing in Freeport, Bahamas with three of my girlfriends. The guy I hooked up with was good in the sack but he came first, then stretched out in my bed. I politely told him,

I don't know what you're going to do to please me, but you're not done. Well, his erection was not returning any time soon. He started performing oral copulation until I was sexually satisfied. Now, my girlfriend was in the bed next to us. She told me the next day that it took everything inside of her not to bust out laughing. This same guy, hopped a flight from Freeport to Fort Lauderdale where I was staying the night of my departure from the Bahamas. I didn't know he was coming to visit me, but we had an amazing time! He made sure I knew he could satisfy me with his dick.

Some men do not want to suck at pleasing a woman. More women should try holding their man to higher sexual standards. The one thing the male ego does not want is a woman deflating it by telling her girlfriends he's horrible in bed.

The Kegel tips I shared in this chapter were provided to help women understand the power of their pussies. Among the reasons that men want to sexually suppress women is due to that fact that they don't want virgins to know they can experience great orgasms without them. Guys don't give a fuck when women who have had their children still have not experienced orgasm. Most men are clueless.

If you knew your vagina could go from zero to a hundred in sixty seconds, you'd be more confident. Well, it can. The average woman can climax in sixty seconds. The average woman can also have an hour-long orgasm. This is a repeat. I know. But wanted to mention it again.

Squirting is also something that 90% of women can do but only 10% have experienced. Keep doing your Kegels. You might get there. Learn to relax and push during sex. Squirting, having an orgasm, and climaxing are three different things.

I'll explain.

Orgasm is the feel-good state you experience. A woman (and man) can stay in the orgasmic stage for well over an hour. A woman can continuously release bodily fluids during the orgasmic state of having mini-orgasms. Sometimes it's off and on. It can be a cool, flowing sensation inside the vagina and/or from the clitoris.

Climaxing is the peak of orgasm when your body releases a bolt of energy. Many women scream! Jerk. Shiver. Tremble uncontrollably, and release bodily fluids inside the vagina and/or from the clitoris.

Squirting or female ejaculation simulates a man's ejaculation. Often a woman's ejaculation is stronger than a man's and has more fluid. Some women can squirt across the room. Every female does not squirt the same. Some females are gushers and release like someone opened the flood gate and poured a gallon of water between her thighs. Other women get super wet as though someone turned on a faucet and there's a continuous slow stream of fluids.

A lot of women experience a urination sensation during sex. They stop and go to the restroom to release themselves. In many cases, she's releasing ejaculate fluid and if she'd kept going, she would've squirted, not urinated. Some women also ejaculate retrograde, meaning the fluids are forced or travel in the opposite direction. This usually happens when a woman tenses up as opposed to relaxing.

Ladies, you should know that your body is like a smart phone—it's complicated. Just as the Bartholin glands secret lubrication to allow a man to penetrate you, the bladder cuts itself off during intercourse (the same is true with men).

Men only have one secretion point. They do not cum and urinate at the same time. Same is true during female ejaculation.

Dicks are Dumb

The urethra can release a clear and odorless ejaculate fluid during sex.

Your G-spot plays a key role in female ejaculation. When stimulated, your G-spot swells with ejaculate fluid. You can learn to squirt on your own, but it's easier (or better) with a man pleasuring you.

When it comes or cums to the G-Spot, some common mistakes men make are: 1) Jabbing his finger repeatedly inside the vagina pushes the ejaculate fluid in the opposite direction; 2) Not knowing where the G-spot is located, he strokes all around it; and 3) Not knowing how to properly do the *come-hither* motion inside the vagina to stimulate the G-Spot.

So where exactly is this mysterious love button located? Ladies, to find out, you can follow these steps in the tub or in bed with your man. Relax while laying on your back. Insert a either G-Spot stimulator or two to three notches of the middle finger inside the vagina. Stroking in a *come-hither* continuous motion, the guy is feeling for tissue that is slightly softer than the rest.

Slide the tip of your tongue along the roof of your mouth all the way back, then move your tongue side-to-side. The G-spot feels like the soft spot. On each side of the G-spot there are what I call trenches. Sometimes a woman responds more when a man strokes to the left or right side of her G-spot.

Once a guy feels this area swelling, he should drag two fingers (middle and pointing or middle and ring) toward him while pressing down (again toward him) at the top of the woman's pubic area. It's like he's trying to pull the fluids out of her.

Some women climax best with their hips elevated. Putting a pillow under your lower back allows a man to better stimulate your G-spot.

Get away from the bed. Standing with the guy behind or in front of you, elevate one foot on a stepstool or chair. Sit on the kitchen countertop, open wide, and let him in. Don't hesitate to stroke your clit while he's penetrating you, ladies.

Whatever you do, be safe and enjoy great sex!

Once a woman becomes sexually liberated, good dick is mandatory.

Recommended Reading:
I'd Rather Be With You by Mary B. Morrison

16
The Mistress Gets Perks

All men do not cheat. Neither are all men liars. There are decent, successful, attractive, married, and single men in relationships that have side chicks. Often the mistress is not a fly by night kind of female that he just wants to have sex with. In many cases, she's his companion. And hard as it is to believe, some men are in-love with their mistress.

For guys who cheat, if his woman could stop him, she would. She can't. How can anyone hold the mistress or side accountable when it's the man who pursues her. The guy gets the erection? The man pulls out his penis. The dude penetrates the woman. It doesn't matter who says "yes" first when two consenting adults engage in intimacy and/or intercourse.

HoneyBHonest: Adultery happens.

Regardless of the lies a man tells, it's never just sex between him and his mistress/side. It's a relationship. He sees her because he wants to. She's with him because she enjoys him.

To the mistresses and sides, I say, "If you're going to allow a married or single man in a relationship into your head, heart, and home, make sure he's fulfilling all your needs, including monetary.

I could tell women it's wrong to date someone else's man, but they already know that. The man knows it too. In reality, people may not be able to control to whom they are attracted, but they choose who they want to fuck.

There are other situations where the man just wants to fuck a female (or male) outside his relationship. One and done! Maybe twice he'll hit if he's on vacation or out of town on business. These men want new pussy, not another woman.

Even in this situation, the woman must know and receive what she wants before taking off her panties. She does not mean anything to him. Why did he have sex with her, if he never wants to get together with her again? That's the question only he knows the correct answer to.

Dicks are dumb but is there ever justification for infidelity? Absolutely.

Married women, females in long-term relationships— you don't have to agree with me on the message I am sharing in this chapter. I'm not condoning cheating—I am simply trying to get more women to understand that all types of men have mistresses and sides. Men fuck because most know they can get away with it. Some feel entitled to lagniappe pussy. While his woman/wife hopes he'll never sex another woman, he's praying he never gets caught.

Let's get this straight, ladies. *Forsaking all others* is a unilateral vow. So is *for better or for worse*. Denying your partner sex for an unreasonable amount of time and expecting them to be faithful is ridiculous. Women are going to lose the "hold out," round almost every time. Just remember, most dicks refuse to be lonely.

For men, cheating and expecting your woman/wife to remain faithful is bananas. Many men won't marry a promiscuous woman. The guy worries that if/when he fucks up, she'll do the same. I tell men, "If you're fucking. I'm fucking." And I mean that.

Stop letting men use you, ladies. If he wants his mistress/side, let him have them. He's going to do it with or without your permission anyway. She knows who you are. Shouldn't you know who she is? The woman your man is fucking, probably raw, knows your kids, where you work, how much you make, your family, friends, etc. She knows these things because your man/husband tells her. Trust me, I know men share more of their personal business than women.

I have a male friend that says he has to have a main and a side. He no longer tells the side he's in a relationship fearing the side—get this—may not fall in love with him if she knows she's a side. He needs both women to love him. Does he love them? No.

The same guy complains that the side never offers and always expects him to pay for everything. He replaced her with another side. Eventually, his main left him and now he's with the latest side but the handwriting is on the wall so to speak. Soon this main will become the side.

It's not us. It's men. A lot of them are fucked up in the heads.

One can argue that my friend is wrong, but men traditionally know what they want from a woman. They often leave women broken and move on to the next in search of what they cannot find in themselves— and that's love and happiness.

HoneyBHonest: Most men do not love themselves. How can they ever love you?

I don't think my friend would ever be happy by himself. Good, bad, or indifferent, users need someone to use.

Men are going to have mistresses, sides, situationships, extras, whatever. If he wants her, he's going to do her.

I'm a proponent for sides and mistresses demanding—yes, demanding whatever they want and getting it upfront, not on the back end. If the man does not agree to provide for the mistress, he should get out of the game and go home to his wife. Perks before panties, ladies.

Recommended Reading:
If You Don't Know Me by Mary B. Morrison

17
Divorcing the Dick

Men remarry faster than women.
Just like a child needs their mother's love, men need to be loved. No matter how big of an asshole he may be in the marriage, he's afraid to start over. First, he's angry with the wife. Everything is her fault. Then he has a "I-don't-give-a-fuck" attitude.

Men want their wife to suffer if she leaves him, but he doesn't understand she's leaving because she was suffering while she was with him. Regardless of how awful a man treats his wife, he never expects her to divorce him.

Guys know they're wrong, but long as women let them have their way, they'll stay. Some dicks want out of the marriage, but the man inside of them never own their shit.

Ladies, if you want out of a bad marriage, develop a plan, in your head. I did say *bad* marriage. What do you need to leave? If it's furniture, do like one of my female friends. Rent a storage unit, start buying and stocking everything you need for your new place so you don't have to start over.

Of course, every woman should have a bank account, or even better, a safety deposit box with cash in it. If you man is spending his and your money on sides, why shouldn't you pay yourself first?

If you have children, how are you going to transition their lifestyles? That's usually the hardest part if your kids are old enough to understand what's happening. If they're grown and you want to leave, go!

All I'm suggesting is, women do not have to live in misery while their husband freely fucks whomever he wants. Those days need to be long gone. It's time for women to cum up!

HoneyBHonest: Women are too nice.

In a divorce, some men have no problem taking all of his wife's money, the house, the car, everything except the kids. It doesn't matter if he contributed to the household or not, he wants to maintain his lifestyle to attract more women. We've seen this happen with female celebrities who marry down.

If a dick is down, let him stay flaccid. A woman picking, holding, or lifting a man up will not make him faithful. The sooner a woman lets go of dead weight, the better.

He needs her coins so he won't skip a beat as he tramples over his soon-to-be ex-wife, to get to all the pussy he can handle, which probably isn't much. The first few women a newly divorced man encounters will be his rebounds. He's quick to say, "I'm fresh out of a marriage. I'm not looking for a serious relationship". All he's ready to do is ejaculate his frustrations inside of multiple women— not caring about any of them. Inside, he's angry, mad, disgusted with women. He needs to purge his ex from his system.

I don't recommend ladies engage in intercourse with recently divorced men.

Focusing on the females, you must understand that a man's ego is fragile. Even if you fake it, don't be a cry lady. Learn to mask your emotions when going through a divorce. Protect your heart. How? By ignoring your man's ego.

The male ego needs acknowledgement to thrive. He needs to know you're hurting because you hurt him. Men seldom accept responsibility for their actions or apologize. Often the apology is not authentic. He says what he believes you need to hear in order for you to allow him one more chance to fuck over you.

Ignore him. Focus on yourself and rebuilding your happiness. Society dicktates that women need to take their time before starting a new relationship. Yet, you never hear anyone telling a man to wait. Most guys don't let the ink dry on the dissolution before they have a new (or not so new) woman.

Ladies, you have to decide when you're ready, and please, don't let others influence you. What you don't have to do is stay miserable and lonely while he's moved on to the next woman.

Crying cleanses the soul. Let it out. Bitch. Complain. Vent to your girlfriends, not your kids or you man. Remember to be as cool and level-headed as you can when going through a divorce.

If you need professional help, get it, but be careful with counseling. It's imperative to confide in the right type of counselor. Some are clinically trained and don't deviate from the script. Others have formulated opinions about women based on a socio-economic background. A counselor should never dictate what you should do.

Try hiring a coach. Their responsibility is to help you become your best by supporting your life goals. A coach can measure your success rate. It's like having your own private cheerleader!

Whatever you do to bounce back, make sure you run your race, at your pace, on your track.

It is okay for a woman to balance dating, working, and being a single parent. Men are quick to say "I don't want another man around my kids". Then tell him to keep the kids. What he really means is he doesn't want any man with you.

If you must divorce the dick, find your peace of mind. Smile as often as you can. Everything is temporary. The only question is how temporary is temporary?

Never be ashamed of becoming a divorced woman. I know women who lived in their husband's shadow for so long they lost their identity. Everything was "my husband this, my husband that", and when he divorced her, she felt like a nobody.

HoneyBHonest: Never forget who you are. But you cannot forget what you don't already know.

Hold your head high. Silence his ego. Although he doesn't deserve it, treat him with respect, not love. And move on with your life. Travel. Get a real dog/pet. Start a new business. When he tries to make you feel like you're nothing, shine brighter. Show the world that you are everything.

Remember, you were awesome before you met him.

Always have your own money. Opening a personal account in your mother's name or someone you trust who will not steal from you is a good thing.

I know a wise woman that bought three houses while she was married— one in each of her children's names. She told each of them, "This is not your house, this is my house". When her husband left her for his mistress, she discovered he had over a half million dollars stashed. She got half of his worth, including his retirement benefits. He never knew about the houses. One can say she was wrong. I say she's a boss bitch!

My father told me, "Speedy, always have enough money to leave. There's nothing worse than being in a bad relationship, and you can't afford to get out". I suggest all women do the same.

I have another girlfriend whose story I would like to share. Men randomly deposit thousands of dollars into her bank account. One might automatically think she's fucking them but she's not. Some guys are so lonely, they'll pay for a woman's company, fly them around the world, and send her expensive gifts.

The best way to divorce the man is to divorce his dick.

HoneyBHonest: When you understand the ego, you understand the man.

Recommended Reading: *The Rich Girls Club* by HoneyB

Thanks for reading *Dicks are Dumb: A Woman's Guide to Choosing the Right Man*. I hope the content was inspiring. Please feel free to send comments, inquiries, and subscribe to my newsletter online at www.MaryMorrison.com.

#HoneyBHonest
Don't act like a lady and think like a man.
Act like a bitch and think like a dick.
Happy Life Ladies!